CONVERSATION MARKETING

© Copyright 2006 Ian Lurie.
All rights reserved. No part of this publication may be reproduced, stored in a retrieval system, or transmitted, in any form or by any means, electronic, mechanical, photocopying, recording, or otherwise, without the written prior permission of the author.

Published by Portent Interactive, Inc.

First Edition   06   1

Book design by Jennifer Van West - www.vanwestco.com

Edited by David Caligiuri

PORTENT INTERACTIVE, INC.
651 Strander Boulevard, Suite 105
Seattle, Washington 98188
(206) 575-3740 · www.portentinteractive.com

Note for Librarians: A cataloguing record for this book is available from Library and Archives Canada at www.collectionscanada.ca/amicus/index-e.html
ISBN 1-4120-9224-8

Printed in Victoria, BC, Canada. Printed on paper with minimum 30% recycled fibre. Trafford's print shop runs on "green energy" from solar, wind and other environmentally-friendly power sources.

Offices in Canada, USA, Ireland and UK

Book sales for North America and international:
Trafford Publishing, 6E–2333 Government St.,
Victoria, BC V8T 4P4 CANADA
phone 250 383 6864 (toll-free 1 888 232 4444)
fax 250 383 6804; email to orders@trafford.com
Book sales in Europe:
Trafford Publishing (UK) Limited, 9 Park End Street, 2nd Floor
Oxford, UK OX1 1HH UNITED KINGDOM
phone 44 (0)1865 722 113 (local rate 0845 230 9601)
facsimile 44 (0)1865 722 868; info.uk@trafford.com
Order online at:
trafford.com/06-0978

10 9 8 7 6 5 4 3

Contents

Introduction: Where's the Lettuce? A Conversation Marketing Parable 3
    Select, Don't Accumulate: A Parable 4
    Accumulation Marketing: The Opposite of Conversation Marketing 5
    The Cure for Accumulation: Conversation Marketing 6

1 **What Is Conversation Marketing? In a Nutshell?** 7
    Can I really use Conversation Marketing? Isn't my company too big/small/rich/poor/new/old? 8
    OK, I knew you'd say that. How do I know if Conversation Marketing is right for me? 8
    Why "Conversation Marketing"? 8
    Morgan's Bikes 10
    The Six Rules 13
    Is this just for marketing? 15

2 **Before You Start: Know Your Goals** 17
    Morgan's Bikes: Sell, sell, sell. Or is there something else? 18

3 **Know the Room: Prepare for Your Conversation** 19
    Personas 19
    Morgan's Bikes: Hitting the Road with Personas 20
    The Workflow 22
    Morgan's Bikes: Going with the Flow 22
    The Calls to Action 23
    Morgan's Bikes: Ready... Action! 24

4 **Dress Appropriately: Belonging in the Conversation** 29
    Audience-Focused Design 30
    Morgan's Bikes: Visual Design 37
    Visual Design Matters, First 39

5 **Sound Smart: Avoiding Conversation Stoppers** 41
    Architecture: When and Where You Say It 41
    Code: How You Say It 46

   Contingency Design: Saying You're Sorry 50
   Content: The 800-pound Gorilla 53
   Sound Smart: Making Sense of It All 54

6 MAKE A CONNECTION: CONTINUING THE CONVERSATION 55
   E-mail: Powerful, but Dangerous 56
   RSS and Podcasting: Emerging Options 59
   Morgan's Bikes: Connecting Here, There, and Everywhere 60
   Keep in Touch 61

7 BRAG MODESTLY: POLITE CONVERSATION STARTERS 63
   Why Search Engines? 63
   A Quick Search-Engine Anatomy Lesson: PPC and Natural
    Rankings 64
   Which Words and Phrases? 65
   PPC Guidelines 66
   Natural Search Guidelines 67
   Other Modest Brags 68
   Morgan's Bikes: Morgan Gets Modest 69

8 OBSERVE AND ADJUST: KEEPING THE CONVERSATION GOING 71
   The Basics: Web Traffic Analysis 71
   The Next Step: Knowing What Works — Conversions 76
   Another Step: Business Intelligence 81
   How to Use Analytics: That Adjusting Thing 82
   Beating the Joneses: How Am I Doing Compared to Everyone Else? 84

9 CONVERSATION MARKETING 87
   Real Life 87

  CONCLUSION 91
   Morgan's Bikes: Story Conclusion 91
   Select, Converse, Don't Accumulate 91

  ACKNOWLEDGMENTS 93

INTRODUCTION
Where's the Lettuce?
A Conversation Marketing Parable

Internet marketing. Did your nose just wrinkle when you read those two words? Just a little? Something smells bad, the same way you feel just a little guilty grabbing all the free stuff at a trade show, or snitching a french fry from your kid's plate.

Internet marketing feels just a little, well, dirty. Why? Because most internet marketing is greedy, not smart, and it leaves the agencies that practice it, and their clients, tarnished.

Typical internet marketing revolves around a drive to get more traffic, no matter what. Viral marketing, search marketing, e-mail marketing (not spam), spam, banner ads, pay-per-click marketing — name the method, and 98 percent of marketers use them as blunt instruments in a get-all-the-traffic-and-let-God-sort-it-out kind of way. Never mind whether that traffic represents truly qualified potential customers. Never mind the cost of driving useless traffic. Just keep 'em coming!

Everyone — clients and marketing professionals alike — is to blame for this. We've all said "More traffic!" at least once in our careers. In traditional media — print, television, and such — it made sense to start off with this approach. But internet marketing is different, and much more powerful. It's a two-way street. That means you can converse with your users, and *select* traffic rather than *accumulate* it. That's what this book is about. It's my attempt to demonstrate how you take advantage of the two-way street and start a real conversation with potential internet customers. But first, a brief story about lettuce....

> *Some folks have told me this bit is entertaining and educational. Others have told me it's totally off the subject. If you're a cut-to-the-chase kind of person, you can skip ahead to chapter 1, "What Is Conversation Marketing? In a Nutshell?"*

Select, Don't Accumulate: A Parable

The concept of "Select, don't accumulate" is the foundation of Conversation Marketing.

Here's my parable that helps explain it: Let's imagine there are two farmers' markets, right next door to each other, and you're shopping for a head of lettuce.

You see a sign, YES, WE HAVE LEAFY GREEN VEGETABLES, and head into that market. It's huge, and really quite striking. You can enter this market through forty or fifty doorways. Once inside, there are thousands of stalls, neatly side by side, all clamoring for attention. Fruits, vegetables, and foodstuffs of every kind, all perfectly formed, brightly colored, ready-for-the-film-shoot little packages of nutritional goodness. Next to each stall are lists of the awards this market has won for design and layout. It's like walking through a food museum. It's great.

But you can't find the damned lettuce. And neither can anyone else. In fact, they're not even sure they *have* lettuce in there. They have cabbage, kale, and some spinach that would make a rabbit swoon, but no lettuce. You're walking around with thousands of other people, trying to find what you need, but no dice. Even worse for the business owners, there are thousands *more* people outside, trying to get in to buy spinach and cabbage and kale, but they can't, because all the lost lettuce-seekers have filled up the store. You finally fight your way out, exasperated.

As you leave, you see a new sign outside, YES, WE HAVE LETTUCE. You follow the arrows, warily, into a different market. This market doesn't gleam quite like the other one. It all looks edible, delicious, even, but the stalls aren't shiny, and the products aren't quite as platonically perfect.

But guess what? You see lettuce. Right in front of you. All kinds of lettuce. Big lettuce, small lettuce, lettuce that looks like famous people. You find what you want, buy it, and you're done.

What just happened? The first market was gleaming, perfect in every way. But you didn't stick around, and you didn't buy anything. Instead, you bought from the other, perfectly functional but infinitely less glamorous market.

It's obvious: The Decent Market's farmers told you they had what you needed, showed it to you, and then you bought it. They conducted very efficient marketing based on what you, the consumer, want. The Gorgeous Market sucked you in, then disappointed you.

Put another way, the Decent Market selected you as a good potential customer, and understood what you really wanted. The farmers of the Gorgeous Market are simply accumulating as many passersby as they can in the hopes of getting lucky.

Accumulation Marketing: The Opposite of Conversation Marketing

Internet marketing seems stuck in hey-want-a-cheap-watch mode: Get people to your site, then worry about whether they really want to be there, or whether they'll buy, or vote, or inquire, or anything else. And accumulation marketing doesn't have to be in-your-face. It takes many other, more subtle forms, too:

CAMPAIGNS THAT OVERGENERALIZE. I've had clients ask me to build "feminine" web sites because women will be their primary audience. Clearly that doesn't work. What if 75 percent of the women coming to the site don't like feminine design (whatever that means)? And what if they're wrong, and half the visitors are men? Or what if they're right, but they still alienate the 25 percent of their audience who are men? The resulting site would draw visitors because of the product, then lose them because of ill-matched content and a design that makes incorrect assumptions. A campaign built this way will accumulate lots of traffic but fail to select the best potential customers.

CAMPAIGNS THAT ARE EGO-DRIVEN. A major manufacturer just revamped their web site. The old site, while not all that attractive, provided clear, fast access to all of their products. The new site, though, opens with a huge Flash animation that takes you on a tour of their facility. It actually shows you what kind of car the CEO drives (and no, they don't make cars). If you wait for the Flash animation to load, and then really examine the home page, you can find your way to their products. Frankly, I don't care about their facility. I want to see the goods. So do the thousands of others who search for and find this manufacturer's site, every day. I'm sure the CEO is very proud of his web site. So is the design firm that built it. But as a communications tool, it's an accumulation-marketing tactic. People come to the site expecting one thing, and they see another.

Accumulation marketing is not based on selection of potential customers. It's relatively indiscriminate, leaving businesses and consumers frustrated. It grows out of broad assumptions about audience and strategy that are both unsubstantiated and inaccurate. Because of that, accumulation marketing can rack up serious traffic numbers and fail utterly to generate any useful business.

The Cure for Accumulation: Conversation Marketing

Accumulation marketing is bad, and it's common. But you can fix it by practicing good Conversation Marketing. So repeat after me:

I will **Select**. *I will* **Converse**. *I will no longer* **Accumulate**.

Say it again:

I will SELECT. I will CONVERSE. I will no longer ACCUMULATE.

The rest of this book will walk you through one strategy to select your audience and make the most of their attention. I call that strategy *Conversation Marketing*. Conversation Marketing ensures that you know your audience, target them with an appropriate message, and then observe their response and adjust that message accordingly. It can do this because of the two-way nature of the internet.

What Is Conversation Marketing? In a Nutshell?

The internet is the only two-way marketing medium outside of a face-to-face meeting, a telephone call, or a video conference. That uniqueness makes internet marketing more efficient, profitable, and much, much more complex.

I've grappled with that for a while now. This book started out as a short piece I was going to give to my staff and clients as an explanation of what we do for a living. It grew into what you're holding now.

If you have this book in your hands, you may feel that your internet marketing isn't quite working, or you may just want to refine what you're doing. The most common mistake folks make when marketing on the internet is treating it like any other medium. Conversation Marketing is a way to address that because it's a strategy that builds on the fact that the internet is a two-way dialogue between you and your audience.

Conversation Marketing is a strategy for meeting age-old marketing challenges on the internet. It's a methodology that makes use of the changes brought about by new, faster, more interactive media, without discarding the basic, sound principles of good communications.

It also ties together creative marketing, web design, copywriting, and the geekiest aspects of web analytics in a way that not only makes sense but provides a blueprint for long-term internet strategies. It's where the internet's technical and communications strengths come together that Conversation Marketing really takes root.

Can I really use Conversation Marketing? Isn't my company too big/small/rich/poor/new/old?

In the past few years, I've seen Conversation Marketing generate a return for labor unions, mom-and-pop businesses, dress designers, companies that sell bulletproof vests, law firms, and consultants. The principles scale well and work for all manner of organizations.

OK, I knew you'd say that. How do I know if Conversation Marketing is right for me?

Folks who have used CM to good effect generally:

- **HAVE AN ARGUMENT TO MAKE**, whether that argument is "Our product is best" or "We can help you improve your life," or even "We know kaizen."
- **ARE READY TO COMMIT FOR THE LONG TERM.** Conversation Marketing requires an investment of time, and doesn't stop when you rebuild a web site. You have to spend time *observing*, *adjusting*, and *refining* what you do.
- **KNOW THEIR LIMITATIONS.** Our best case studies come from folks who work with internet professionals to implement their plan. Sounds like a sales pitch, I know. But I'll bet most of you don't sew your own clothes before you go to a party. And if you do, you don't drive there in a car you built yourself. And you learned to speak one or more languages with the help of others, right? You get my point....

Why "Conversation Marketing"?

A conversation is, at a minimum, a two-way exchange of information — I talk, you listen and respond. I hear your response and answer accordingly, and you do the same, and so on, until the conversation concludes.

Think about traditional marketing media. In print, you deliver an advertisement to your readers, who read it and decide whether to contact you or not. You have no way to know whether they read that ad — you only know if it works if someone calls you and says, "Hey, I saw your ad, and I'd like to buy from you." Measurement is tough, and there's no way to change your message, in the short term, according to audience response. On the radio, it's about the same, and television is even harder to change.

In other words, marketing in traditional media is *not* a conversation. Information is delivered, but there's no observe-and-respond cycle. You can't quickly adjust to your audience's needs, wants, or approval/disapproval of your initial message.

Now consider the internet. You deliver a message to your audience via web site, ad on another web site, or e-mail marketing piece. Folks see your message, and you know they see it because you can measure "views." They click on the ad, a link in the e-mail, or drill deeper into your site, and you know that, because you can measure that, too. Then they do or do not take the action you want them to take (buy, join, rent, sign up, etc.), and you know that, as well, because yes, you can measure *that*, too. And you can do all of this anonymously, at a fraction of the cost of traditional marketing. Most importantly, you can do all of this in *real time*. So you can modify your web site, banner ad, or landing page after days, hours, or even minutes of beginning a campaign. You deliver a message. Your audience responds. You observe and adjust your message accordingly. Bingo, a conversation occurs.

The internet is the first mass-marketing medium where this level of two-way interaction can occur in a polite*, empirically measurable way.

---

* I said "polite." *Of course there are all sorts of not-so-polite conversations on the internet. You can engage in them if you want. We won't judge. But this book isn't about 'em.*

Morgan's Bikes

Here's an example of internet vs. print marketing that further points out the difference between Conversation Marketing and everything else.

Let's take an imaginary business: Morgan's Custom Bikes. Morgan is a sharp businessperson, and she's gotten her company going by building two or three high-priced, custom-built bicycles every month. Now, though, she wants to start making more Morgan Road Specials and selling them all over the country, in local shops. The Road Special is one of those skinny-tire $6,000 high-tech marvels you see in the Tour de France, and there are lots of cyclists drooling to get their hands on just that kind of bike. But local shops won't order her product if customers don't ask for it by name. So she needs to get the word out.

PRINT CAMPAIGN. Morgan starts with a print ad in a major cycling magazine. She takes out a full-page ad, which isn't cheap. The ad is beautiful: a famous Tour de France cyclist, smiling broadly, races down a country road on a Morgan Road Special. The message is clear, "Buy this machine, it's a real treat, and you'll ride like a pro." Her print campaign has all of the earmarks of a successful campaign: celebrity, a strong message, and impressive visuals.

Results are mixed, though. A few orders trickle in, and after a four-month run she barely breaks even on the ad. More importantly, no shops are pre-ordering the Road Special. She keeps it running, but starts pondering alternatives.

INTERNET CAMPAIGN. Morgan already has a web site that features her product, specifications, reviews, and ordering information, so she decides to try to generate a buzz on the internet. She spends a little cash on a banner ad for a road bicycle review web site, buys a pay-per-click ad on a major search engine, and sponsors a popular cycling-news e-mail list for three months (she gets a link and one paragraph about the Road Special for sponsorship). Morgan sees some results right away — three new orders come in after about a week. She reads her web site traffic report and learns that these new orders came from the pay-per-click ad and the e-mail newsletter. The banner isn't generating any traffic at all, much less orders. She spends more money on pay-per-click ads and, after an unproductive month, cancels the banner ad. Her orders increase the moment her pay-per-click links appear on major search engines.

She's doing better, but still not great — no pre-orders — because customer demand just isn't high enough yet. After two months, Morgan reviews her order history, her web traffic logs, and feedback from customers, and realizes five things:

- A lot of folks are clicking on her pay-per-click ads.
- More folks who read the e-mail sponsorship actually order, though.
- Her typical internet-inspired customer is some kind of competitive cyclist.
- Her typical internet customer was visiting her web site on an older computer.
- Very few people call her after their first visit to her site — they need to ponder a bit before plunking down $6,000 on a bicycle.

Armed with this information, she makes some changes:

- Morgan sponsors a second e-mail list, dedicated to those who race bicycles, and pays extra to include some basic information about the Morgan Road Special.
- She simplifies her web site, removing animation and anything else that might slow down an older computer on a slower internet connection.
- She changes all of her e-mail and pay-per-click links to point to a special page on her site that talks about the race handling of the Road Special, and includes testimonials from racers who ride it.
- She modifies her print ad, which is due for renewal, to emphasize her web site.

- She adds an e-mail newsletter of her own, and lets visitors sign up from her web site, so that she can keep in touch with them.

Morgan hits pay dirt. Three bike shops in California call her within a month, asking if they can pre-order the Road Special for sale in their shops. Now she can make more bikes, get more exposure, and expand her company.

WHY THIS WORKED. Morgan's internet efforts were very successful, and even helped her adjust her non-internet campaign. Why? She did a few crucial things. Morgan:

- *Knew the room*: That is, she used results from ongoing marketing efforts to get a clearer picture of her audience. She learned her typical internet visitors were competitive cyclists with older computers (since most competitive cyclists spend all of their money on bicycles). She also learned that they are not impulse buyers. That let her select her audience, rather than accumulate virtual passersby.
- *Dressed appropriately*: As she learned, she modified her web site to better cater to her audience. She added content that would help them make a good decision — positive feedback from other cyclists. She also simplified her site so that her product could speak for itself.
- *Sounded smart*: Morgan changed where her internet ads pointed, so that people clicking on those ads immediately saw information most likely to answer their questions. She also put her ads and sponsorships in the best venues.
- *Made a connection*: Morgan added an e-mail sign-up link to her site, and started sending folks a monthly newsletter. That way she didn't have to rely on them to remember her web address, or the print ad, when they wanted to learn more.
- *Bragged modestly*: Morgan sought out ad venues where she could put herself in front of potential customers in the least intrusive manner. (Note: She forgot about search-engine optimization — we'll talk more about that later.)

She also emphasized testimonials. Basically, Morgan got other folks to brag for her. That's bragging modestly.

- *Observed and adjusted*: She read her site-traffic reports and sales reports. Based on that information she drew conclusions and tweaked her campaign to better reflect what she learned.

The Six Rules

I was sneaky. I just introduced you to the six rules of Conversation Marketing:

KNOW THE ROOM (AKA GET SELECTIVE). When you go to a party, what's the first thing you do? You look around and see if you know anyone. That's a good idea on the internet, too. Try to learn the nature of the people with whom you converse. Knowing the room means knowing what your audience likes and doesn't like, their technological limitations, and a range of other attributes. It means selecting your audience rather than accumulating it. It's the foundation of a good campaign.

DRESS APPROPRIATELY. That's *appropriately*, not *cool*. You don't wear a ripped T-shirt to a black-tie dinner. And you don't wear a tuxedo to a football game. Your web site should know where it's going, too. It should be designed with your audience in mind — classy if elegance will resonate, simple if complexity is a threat, or a multimedia extravaganza if entertainment is paramount. Internet marketing is a communications contest, not a design competition — do what's appropriate.

SOUND SMART. This rule could actually be "Don't sound stupid." If you know the room, and you're dressed appropriately, then you've probably cleared that first, quick inspection by fellow conversationalists. Now you have to actually *converse*. On the internet, that means a few things: you have to deliver good content, in the correct order, and your site has to work. Sounding smart brings together architecture, writing, programming, usability, and contingency design, and these will occupy a lot of our time as we move through this book.

MAKE A CONNECTION. It's great to meet everyone at a party, but you want them to talk to you later on, too. At a party, you exchange business cards or phone numbers. On the internet, you use e-mail or some other technique (such as RSS — if you don't know what that is, do a quick search on the web and you'll find out) to help folks keep in touch with you.

BRAG MODESTLY. At a party, nothing's better than having the host introduce you as "The person I told you about. You *have* to talk to him/her." Someone else just bragged for you — that's modest, but still a great boast. On the internet, modest bragging abounds. Search engines, blogs, and an endless array of PR opportunities allow someone else to say how important you are.

OBSERVE AND ADJUST. A conversation is really millions of near-instant observations and adjustments. If I'm talking to you and you look at me as though I just turned bright yellow, I may change the subject or ask if you're OK. If you laugh, I may tell another joke. Internet marketing is remarkably similar — you can use web site traffic reports and dozens of other measurements to gauge audience response and adjust your efforts, whenever. This is the lynchpin and litmus of successful internet marketing. It is also where I see most organizations fail, miserably, to realize the real promise of internet marketing.

Put these all together and you have a recipe for a selected, interested audience seeing a campaign that they find truly compelling. The rest of this book will explore these six principles in detail, and tie them together. I'll include examples, tools, and, as you read, a step-by-step guide for implementing the six rules in a way that'll realize concrete goals for you and your organization.

Is this just for marketing?

Nope. Conversation Marketing is actually a solid communications strategy for anyone who needs to get a message out. The message might be "Buy this," "Join us," "Vote for me," "I am cooler than you," or just "Have a look."

So why call it *Conversation Marketing*? Most folks using this strategy do so in the context of a marketing/PR campaign in an effort to sell *something*. Also, *Conversation Marketing and Communications and Stuff* sounds pretty silly, don't you think?

Before You Start: Know Your Goals 2

A few words about goals, before we start the Conversation Marketing process: You need to know what you're trying to accomplish, and you need to ask yourself whether your goals are realistic in light of your budget and other constraints.

Think hard — what will it take for you to say that your web site is a "success"? Does it need to reduce the cost of doing business? Help you sell more stuff? Help you grow a distribution channel? Access a new audience for you?

I encourage my clients to start by asking four basic questions:

1. What do I need my web site to accomplish?
2. What is my budget?
3. How quickly do I need this done?
4. In light of the first three answers, can I succeed?

Hold on, you say. How can I define goals when I haven't defined audience, or anything else, yet?

You're right. Your goals will change while you plan, and even after you launch, your web site. But Conversation Marketing is very flexible, and meant to adapt, *if* you get started. You have to establish some basic criteria for success, and make sure that those criteria are reasonable, or you'll never get your project off the ground.

"More traffic" is not a well-defined goal. If you said that, go give yourself a time-out.

Morgan's Bikes: Sell, sell, sell. Or is there something else?

Morgan's Custom Bikes is starting its Conversation Marketing campaign. Morgan sits down to plan, and of course starts with a pretty simple goal: Sell more bikes. But that doesn't seem terribly enlightening, so she tries to narrow things a bit. *What* can her web site do that'll help her sell more?

As she ponders, she realizes her business goals are a little more defined:

- Start and grow a network of bicycle shops that sell her product, both on a custom-made and off-the-shelf basis.
- Grow consumer awareness of the product.
- Get a community of devoted riders who like her product and will someday upgrade to another Morgan's Custom Bikes model.
- Connect potential customers to bicycle shops that sell her product, to make the buying process easier.
- Lower the cost of keeping both dealers and current customers up-to-date on new products and other news.

She also identifies a few things that are *not* goals:

- E-commerce. She doesn't want an online store.
- Any form of online ordering of custom models, even without e-commerce.
- Change to her current system of order processing and delivery.

Sometimes knowing what you don't want to do is just as important. While she has a pretty long list of goals, they're complementary, and by ruling out e-commerce and business process changes, she's set some boundaries for her project.

Morgan knows her budget and thinks that she can at least begin working toward all of her goals from the get-go. Now she's ready to start her Conversation Marketing campaign by making sure she knows the room.

Know the Room: Prepare for Your Conversation 3

Know thy audience. Before I get into that, though, I should explain what "audience" really means.

Your audience is the group you're trying to communicate with and persuade (you're always trying to persuade, even if you're just trying to persuade them to keep listening). Really, awareness of audience requires awareness of three things:

- **Personas.** The attributes that define your audience.
- **Workflow.** The way your audience is most likely to move through your site.
- **Calls to action.** The places in that workflow where there's some specific action you want them to take, such as purchase, sign up, download a white paper, etc.

Personas

First, you need to understand who is going to use your site. To do that, you create broad definitions of the different typical visitors. These definitions are called *personas*.

You can use a lot of different resources to define a persona:

- Sales and other demographic data from existing customers, members, dealers, or other groups.
- Feedback from your own sales force.
- Data purchased from survey firms, marketing agencies, or professional organizations.
- Data gathered in focus groups and from surveys.
- Your gut instinct.
- A million other sources of information — in the interests of saving paper and bits, I'll let you take it from here.

The first person I know of to use this term in a marketing context was Alan Cooper, around 1999. You can learn more about him and his firm at www.cooper.com. He has an excellent newsletter, too.

At a minimum, always look at existing data, get feedback from sales/outreach folks, and rely on gut instinct. Purchased data, surveys, focus groups, and other forms of external or "fresh" information can be priceless, though — if you can, make room in your budget.

Once you've collected your data, build your personas. Expect to have two or three different personas on a particular project. Very few organizations have only one, and if you find there are more than three, you need to reexamine the goals of your project — in nine years I've never seen a web site successfully cater to more than three distinct groups.

A typical persona definition includes:

- **DEMOGRAPHICS OF THE PERSONA.** Average age, level of internet expertise, and spending habits are all characteristics.
- **CONSTRAINTS.** You may run up against this persona's technological limitations (type of internet connection), a language barrier, or even vision impairment.
- **NEEDS AND WANTS.** What are the challenges facing this persona? What solutions do you offer that will turn this persona into a real-life customer? "Have a more comfortable bicycle that also rides faster" might be a goal for a persona on Morgan's Custom Bikes.

You don't have to perfectly know the room, right away. Remember, it's *Conversation* Marketing. You'll learn more about your audience later, and you'll act on what you've learned. Imagine a magazine ad that tells you who's looking and whether they like the ad or not....

Morgan's Bikes: Hitting the Road with Personas

Morgan immediately realizes she has two personas she needs to please:

CONSUMERS are folks who may buy and ride a Road Special. Using her past sales data and a little intuition, she knows that typical consumer-customers race on weekends, but not professionally. They typically work in white-collar jobs, and probably two out of three are men. They're generally very web-literate and buy all sorts of smaller goods online, but they won't want to buy a custom bike without personal attention from a shop owner. Morgan also talks to a few local shops and finds out what they hear from customers looking for high-end road bicycles. They tell her that typical consumers looking for an upscale, custom ride are over thirty and ride regularly with their clubs and groups. And, most importantly, most of these consumers take at least a month to decide which bike to buy.

Morgan wants to please consumers — they buy her product, after all, and they go to shop owners to order. Every consumer whose interest is captured isn't just another potential customer, he's also another voice persuading shop owners to distribute the Road Special.

SHOP OWNERS are established sellers of bicycles, accessories, and repair services. They could be anywhere in the world. Morgan knows that her best dealers run a fairly high-end shop, have a small, dedicated clientele, and are experts in all facets of cycling: equipment, training, and sports trivia. They're huge fans and see their sport as a calling, not just a business — they're passionate about it. Ages vary widely. But most of the time shop owners in or near cities or suburbs have the easiest time selling Morgan's bicycles. And most of the shops already selling her bicycles also carry at least one other custom brand.

These owners want and need products that they can recommend without hesitation. They also want a manufacturer they can trust.

Morgan really wants to please shop owners — they're her ticket to the big time....

These two personas compose Morgan's audience. Now it's time to figure out how to deliver what they want.

The Workflow

Once you know your personas, you have to determine a model for how each persona might use your site. You can do that using *workflows*. A workflow is a simple, commonsense map that describes how a persona moves through a web site — it may include a single visit, but typically spans several, and ends with some desired conclusion.

A workflow might be a simple list, a flowchart, a mind map, or anything else that makes sense to you. When we map out workflows for our customers, we typically use flowcharts that we can later combine to show all personas together (also called swimming lane diagrams, for you process modelers out there), but really anything that makes sense for you will do.

Morgan's Bikes: Going with the Flow

Personas firmly in hand, Morgan can now think about how they might use her site. She starts with the consumer, and does a simple list:

1. Conversation starts: Hear about the Road Special on the web, in print, or from a friend.
2. Arrive at web site.
3. Read about the Road Special on the overview page.
4. If I like it, read the technical specifications and/or the testimonials.
5. Check on the price.
6. Leave the web site. Think it over, talk to my friends, maybe ask a local shop about the bike and what they've heard. Check for reviews on the web.
7. Come back to the web site. Dig deeper — read the specifications if I haven't already. Learn about custom options.
8. Think about the configuration I'd really want.
9. Find out how to order.

10   Leave the web site. Go to my local shop and place an order.
11   Get my bike. Ride it. Love it!
12   A little later, consider upgrades — what else can I do to make my bike cooler?
13   Can I get a jersey/T-shirt/other stuff to show I own a Road Special?

It's that simple. Notice that the workflow isn't necessarily web-centric — a lot of stuff in here might or might not take place on her web site. And it doesn't end with a purchase, either. Upgrades and accessories keep the conversation going.

The Calls to Action

Now you know who's going to use your site, and you've sketched out how. The final step in knowing the room is understanding where in this process opportunities exist to help potential consumers move forward — at some point you have to "sell" them, even if you're just trying to persuade them to sign up for a newsletter or to download a document.

What are you trying to persuade them to do? The possibilities are endless, and "Buy this" is only one, very narrow message. "Elect me," "Sign up for our newsletter," "Have another look," "Download our white paper," and "Take a test drive" are also valid calls. Consider your call to action very, very carefully.

Typically you're going to have several different calls to action. If, for example, you sell something, the ideal call to action is "Make a purchase." But there are other actions your audience can take that will lead to a good outcome. They could sign up for your newsletter, or order a free sample, or tell a friend about your product. Don't depend on folks to take the best possible action the first time they visit your site. Instead, give them options that escalate to that best action.

To figure out your calls to action, think about what you'd do upon first visiting your site. Make an ordered list, or a flowchart, or whatever else works for you, of the things a visitor will do, right up to the best possible action.

This can be the toughest part of knowing the room. A call to action is legitimate only if two basic rules are met:

The call to action addresses a need of one or more personas.
AND
Answering that call to action means a persona does something you want them to do.

Morgan's Bikes: Ready... Action!

Now Morgan thinks about which steps in the conversation offer an opportunity for her to provide something that keeps the conversation going. When in this process might her company help the potential customer and, at the same time, make sure this person keeps Morgan's Bikes in mind? In her case, the obvious points for this are when someone might seek advice from others, when they are configuring their Road Special, and after they buy. At each of these steps, Morgan can provide tools to help the customer. So, she revises her workflow, adding calls to action as follows:

1. Hear about the Road Special on the web, in print, or from a friend.
2. Arrive at web site.
3. Read about the Road Special on the overview page.
4. If I like it, read the technical specifications and/or the testimonials.
5. Check on the price.
6. Leave the web site. Think it over, talk to my friends, maybe ask a local shop about the bike and what they've heard. Check for reviews on the web.
   ACTION: E-MAIL A FRIEND.

7   Come back to the web site. Dig deeper — read the specifications if I haven't already. Learn about custom options.
    ACTION: CONTACT MORGAN'S CUSTOM BIKES.
8   Think about the configuration I'd really want.
    ACTION: REGISTER, SAVE CONFIGURATION, AND E-MAIL A FRIEND.
9   Find out how to order.
10 Leave the web site. Go to my local shop and place an order.
    ACTION: FIND A DEALER, SEND CONFIGURATION TO THEM FROM SITE.
11 ACTION: GET MY BIKE. RIDE IT. LOVE IT!
    ACTION: JOIN THE ROAD SPECIAL CLUB. OPT IN FOR NEWSLETTER.
12 A little later, consider upgrades — what else can I do to make my bike cooler?
13 Can I get a jersey/T-shirt/other stuff to show I own a Road Special?

Morgan has found six basic calls to action:

- E-MAIL A FRIEND: Send a page of her web site, or a saved configuration, to a friend.
- CONTACT US: Of course, anyone might contact Morgan directly to learn more. Never overlook this call to action — direct contact remains one of the best selling tools, and the internet is unique in its ability to facilitate this.
- REGISTER: Potential customers can provide a little personal info and create an account. Then they can save the configuration of their custom Road Special.
- FIND AND CONTACT A DEALER: Once they've decided to buy, or before, registered customers can send their configuration directly to an authorized dealer in their area.
- BUY A ROAD SPECIAL.

- JOIN THE ROAD SPECIAL CLUB: Sign up for an opt-in e-mail newsletter.

These steps can show up anywhere on the site. "E-mail a friend" should probably be available on every page, as should the e-mail newsletter sign-up.

The most important thing to note, though, is that "Buy a Road Special" is only one of five possible outcomes that can help Morgan's company. For example, if visitors contact dealers, this is good for the company even if those visitors don't buy. Why? Because dealers are another audience for her.

If potential customers contact dealers, those dealers learn that there's possible demand for her product, and are that much more likely to recommend her product to other customers or to call her on their own.

By figuring out these calls to action, Morgan now knows there are some tools she needs to include on her site:

These calls to action also present opportunities to measure audience response. We'll talk more about that when we discuss "Observe and Adjust" in chapter 8.

- An opt-in e-mail newsletter.
- A bike configurator, so that visitors can pick options and then save their ideal Road Special.
- A dealer-search-and-contact tool, so that visitors who are ready to buy can easily find a shop.
- "E-mail a friend," so that visitors can easily forward pages on her site to their friends.

Let's try this exercise again, with a different audience. Morgan really has at least two audiences — while she wants consumers to buy her bikes, her real goal is to get local shops to sell her bikes en masse. She maps out a shop owner workflow, and includes calls to action:

STEP	CALL TO ACTION	SITE FEATURE
1 Learn about the Road Special from a customer, magazine, trade show, or the web.		
2 Go to the web site to learn more.		
3 Check out possible options and configurations.		
4 Decide whether I would like this bike or not. Can I sell it to my customers and feel good about it?	CONTACT OTHER DEALERS FOR REFERENCES.	*Get permission from current dealers to give out their contact information. If yes, let prospective dealers contact them.*
5 Figure out: Is there demand? If not, can I create demand for this bike?	CHECK SEARCH DATA — ARE CYCLISTS SEARCHING FOR DEALERS IN MY AREA?	*Ask prospective dealers to register on the site. Provide a link to customer search data so they can see demand.*

Note that this time Morgan used a more organized format, with the workflow steps on the left, the call to action in the middle, and the site feature needed to answer that call to action on the right. This format is one of my favorites.

STEP	CALL TO ACTION	SITE FEATURE
6 Find how to become a reseller — what programs does Morgan's offer me?	CONTACT MORGAN'S WITH QUESTIONS, AND REGISTER FOR DEALER-SHIP INFORMATION.	*Provide contact form. Also provide dealer registration form online.*
7 Now I'm a dealer. I want to do the best job selling this product.	KEEP IN TOUCH WITH MORGAN'S.	*Provide an opt-in e-mail newsletter for all registered dealers.*

So, Morgan now knows with *whom* she's trying to converse. She's sketched out *how* they will likely want to converse. And she's identified *where* this communication offers opportunities to move the conversation forward. Time to make sure her web site will be dressed appropriately.

4

DRESS APPROPRIATELY: BELONGING IN THE CONVERSATION

If you know your audience, you can wear the right clothes to the party. Ever go to a beach party wearing a three-piece suit? Or end up at a black-tie dinner in jeans? Makes you uncomfortable just thinking about it, doesn't it?

In any conversation, first impressions matter — at a party and on the internet. In a social environment, folks are more likely to talk to you if you fit their expectations of a good conversationalist. When people arrive at your site they're going to make a near-instant decision as to whether you have what they need. Most site visitors will process elements of the site's design in this order:

1. Colors
2. Textures and effects
3. Typefaces
4. Complexity
5. Layout and positioning

Conversation Marketing can only start once a visitor has unconsciously moved through this checklist.

How do you make sure your web site is dressed appropriately? For starters, let's break down the phrase *Dress Appropriately*:

- **DRESS**, in this case, means the appearance of your web site. That's a really complex concept, but we'll keep it simple for the moment.
- **APPROPRIATELY** means catering to and delivering an experience expressly designed for your audience. "Appropriately" does not necessarily mean "cool." And "audi-

ence" means your *audience*. Not *you*. More rants about this later.

I'll warn you now that this chapter is as much about what not to do as it is about what you should do. For me, at least, design is as much an exercise in avoiding pitfalls as it is a creative act.

This chapter is not a course in web site design. Nor is it an attempt to set broad boundaries for what's "good" or "bad" web design. It's designed to make you an educated judge of "good" versus "bad" design in the context of an individual internet marketing campaign: "good" being a design that quickly connects with your intended audience and ushers them into a deeper conversation; "bad" being a design that either fails to make that connection or actually breaks it. I can't give you a great checklist. But if there's one thing you should do, it's this: Always practice audience-focused design. Real-life conversations are painful when one person ignores the other's likes and dislikes, and Conversation Marketing is no different.

Audience-Focused Design

You put a lot of time into knowing the room, right? Pondered your audiences, considered calls to action, mapped out workflows, and generally tied yourself up in knots trying to anticipate the who, how, and why of your Conversation Marketing campaign.

Now you put that all to work, by creating a "look" that will appeal to the personas created in rule 1, *and* make it easy for them to use your site. By doing that, you'll make sure that the conversation gets started.

Remember, a conversation isn't just about what you like. It's about the other person, too. Conversation Marketing works the same way. Your web site's look and feel isn't about what *you* like. You already like your business, most likely. You're probably already excited about the product or service or message you're delivering. You don't have to persuade yourself.

Designs created to please the business owner are what I call ego driven, rather than audience focused. Don't get me started....

The first goal of your web site is to get a first-time visitor to stay just long enough to start reading or viewing your message — to start the conversation. No more, no less. That means that the first thing they see has to evoke the right response.

Now, I said I can't give you a "good design" checklist. But there are a few basic aspects of a web site's look that I've found can be conversation starters, and stoppers.

Colors

Nothing starts, or stops, a conversation faster than a bright green shirt, right? Same goes for your web site.

People react certain ways to certain colors. Here are some examples:

RED	Excitement, high energy, warmth, caution, exercise, aggression
NAVY BLUE	Stability, calm, professionalism, maturity, science
GREEN	Progress, nature, action, comfort, arts
BROWN	Earth, accessibility, outdoors
YELLOW	Energy, caution, good, outdoors, exercise
ORANGE	Emotion, nature, heat, sunlight, fire
PURPLE	Youth, superiority, femininity, aggression
PINK	Femininity, welcoming, warmth, passivity
WHITE	Purity, cleanliness, ease, trust, creativity, newness
BLACK	Seriousness, the avant-garde, weight, gravity, age, entertainment
GRAY	Neutrality, calm, maturity, integrity, warrior

These are all value judgments — different cultures may interpret colors in very different ways. But in my middle-class North American experience, these responses hold true on sites that present everything from politics to dresses.

When someone arrives at your web site, color will typically be the first thing that evokes a response. Whether they see a splash of red in a photograph, or the background color used in the overall layout, that first bit of color will drive their experience. So you need to select colors carefully.

One other note about color: Think about usability. A measurable percentage of the male population has a form of shade blindness that makes it very difficult for them to see, for example, blue text on a red background — don't laugh, I've seen a lot of sites with this color scheme.

If you want to play it safe with color, make sure your web site follows these basic guidelines:

- *Always opt for high contrast between the background and text color.*
- *Use dark-colored text on a light-colored background.* This isn't a must, but people are used to it and it's the safest route.
- *Don't use colors that evoke a strong response unless you want one.* Bright reds, yellows, and purples will get an immediate "Cool!" or "Eck!" from your audience. If you want more time to persuade them, stick to grays, softer blues, browns, and other earth tones.
- *If you don't want the colors to take center stage, stick to those that occur in nature: brown, green, etc.* We're used to seeing these shades and can easily process information against this kind of backdrop.

Textures and Effects

Do you like beveled buttons? Drop shadows? Metallic, shiny shapes on your computer screen? C'mon, don't be embarrassed.

Texturing and effects have their place even if many designers and marketers turn their noses up at the idea of a drop shadow. Used correctly they can help emphasize a point, isolate a message, or make a web site more usable.

But you have to have a reason for applying effects. And "Because I like them" doesn't count. If you sell a high-tech product, then a shiny, three-dimensional web site may make sense. If you sell socks, though, you'd best reconsider.

Here are some examples of effects, and the responses they evoke:

BEVELING	*Technology, emphasis, convention*
SHINE	*Technology, fiction/fantasy, the avant-garde, aggression*
DROP SHADOW	*Emphasis, subtlety, arts*
GRADIENT FILLS	*Creativity, arts*
ROUNDED CORNERS	*Softness, femininity, creativity*

Used in combination with different colors, effects can elicit very subtle or very strong responses. If your web site incorporates any kind of effect, have a good reason. Again, "This is cool" is *not* enough. Effects should help the visitor get your point. They shouldn't *be* the point.

Let me put it another way: Nothing should be on your web page without a good reason. If a button or effect isn't helping to keep the conversation going, get rid of it. Ever know anyone who used one particular word they liked over and over again, whether it was relevant or not? Did it make you want to scream? Well, having every inch of a web page covered with beveling can be just as unpleasant.

One more thing: Expertise is everything, here. Only someone who truly understands design principles can apply effects to a web site's look without risking grating, painful results.

Typefaces

Type and typesetting are a critical part of dressing appropriately. Your visitor has now arrived at your site — in the first fractions of a second he's processed the colors and textures you used. Now he's going to see if there's anything to read. He's not going to *read* it, yet, but his eyes are already tracking the page, looking for cues and calls to action. Choosing fonts is like deciding whether to speak loudly or softly, quickly or slowly, or to use big words or small ones. This choice is fundamental to Conversation Marketing.

Fonts aren't just for reading. They're shapes and lines that can generate as strong a response as splotches of color. And how they're applied to a page can have equally strong implications for your site.

First, there's the difference between *serif* and *sans serif* fonts.

Times Roman is a serif font — basically, serifs are the little feet you see at the bottom and top of each letter. They create an ornate, artistic look. Serif fonts are the norm in print — if you buy a paperback book, chances are it uses one serif family or another. So do most newspapers. Serif fonts are harder to read on a computer screen, but they definitely have a place, and some serif families out there are more subtle and easier to read in a digital environment.

Use serif typefaces if you're trying to create a literary, artistic, or classic feel. Try to avoid them if you're aiming for a techy feel.

Arial is sans serif font. It's all clean lines, and doesn't have any of the extra adornments. Sans serif fonts create a crisp, direct look. They're easier to read on a computer screen, and provide a more technical, unpretentious feel. While the average reader doesn't run into sans serif fonts on the printed page, he or she is generally more comfortable with them online. Use sans serif fonts to appeal to the broadest possible audience. If your Conversation Marketing campaign is dealing with a wide audience who needs to get in, get their question answered, and get out, use san serif fonts.

How you treat type on the page matters, too. I can't begin to offer a complete primer on typesetting — see your local bookstore for some great books on the subject — but here are a few pointers.

LINE SPACING MATTERS. By default, web browsers display lines of text with very tight spacing (also called *leading*). That's harder to read.

Here's some text with tight leading. It's like talking really fast:

> Lorem ipsum dolor sit amet, consectetuer adipiscing elit. Morbi commodo, ipsum sed pharetra gravida, orci magna rhoncus neque, id pulvinar odio lorem non turpis. Nullam sit amet enim.

Here's some text with looser leading. Notice the difference. It feels like the page is talking more slowly.

> Lorem ipsum dolor sit amet, consectetuer adipiscing elit.
>
> Morbi commodo, ipsum sed pharetra gravida, orci magna
>
> rhoncus neque, id pulvinar odio lorem non turpis. Nullam
>
> sit amet enim

LETTER SPACING MATTERS, TOO. Applying additional space between letters in a phrase will create emphasis for navigation cues, headings, and such. Don't do this too much though or it looks like you're yelling:

> T H I S   T E X T   H A S   L O O S E R   L E T T E R   S P A C I N G

Go very, very sparingly with boldface, italics, and underscoring.

STICK TO CONVENTIONS. For example, visitors automatically think "hyperlink" when they see underscored text. Don't stray too far if you want to have wide appeal.

Here's a quick reference for typographical principles and faux pas:

SERIF FONTS	*Classical, complex, literary, pithy*
SAN SERIF FONTS	*Clear, open, simple, accessible*
UNDERSCORING	*"Click here."*
DIFFERENT COLOR	*"Click here."*
WIDE LETTER SPACING	*"Important!"*

Really great typography is an art form. I know just enough to keep you from putting your virtual foot in your mouth. If you want to read some great articles on the subject, visit A List Apart: http://www.alistapart.com/topics/design/typography/.

ORNATE, CURLY FONTS	*"The site owner really likes fancy fonts."*
BOLD	*"Important!" if used sparingly.*
	"Bad web site!" if used too much.

In any conversation, the way you present your words is important. In Conversation Marketing it's crucial, because it sets the tone for the entire conversational chain of events. Use the wrong font or overuse a text effect and it's like showing up at a beach party in a tuxedo. You will *not* be dressed appropriately.

Complexity

The number of columns, shapes, text blocks, images, and other widgets you include on a page all pertain to complexity. So does any use of motion graphics, such as Flash.

Not much to say here — the more complex your page is, the more you can communicate. A simpler layout will do more to emphasize a single message or theme. A more complex layout, on the other hand, lets you say a lot more in the same space.

If your audience is looking for convenience — if they're looking to you to make something easier for them — you need to keep things simple. The same holds true if your audience is less experienced with the internet.

If, on the other hand, your audience is looking for lots of information, is made up of experienced internet users, or is generally techier, you can create a more complex layout and let them explore.

Layout and Positioning

The Occidental eye takes in a page of information in a Z shape or some derivative.

Items at the corners of the page are emphasized. Items at the top left and bottom right will be the first and last things visitors see when they first scan the page. The top left corner is by far the most viewed, most studied part of any page.

Does that mean the most important stuff needs to be at the top left and bottom right? No. It does mean, though, that you need to consider what you put there. If you put a bright graphic, boldface type, or something that's otherwise an attention-grabber in either of those locations, it's going to dominate the page. In conversational terms, think of it as standing on a podium with a microphone.

The Golden Rule

Dozens of books have been written about graphic design. And a few designers have made their way in the world based purely on their ability to create a striking online aesthetic. But in my experience, the visual design of your site matters for about 15 to 20 seconds. In that time, a visitor decides whether they're going to stay or leave.

In the marketing context, web design is about that first 20 seconds. A great-looking design is like dressing appropriately — it gets folks to accept you long enough to hear what you have to say.

So the Golden Rule of web design is: *Design for your audience*. In Conversation Marketing, that will let you talk *to* your audience, instead of *at* them.

Morgan's Bikes: Visual Design

Morgan is a pretty creative sort. She decides to design the Morgan's Custom Bikes home page on her own. Her first design features a huge, high-resolution image of a local team racing around a curve, all on shiny new Road Specials. It's a beautiful, striking image, and she follows it up with internal site pages that are dominated by additional original photos.

Morgan passes the pages off to a web developer, who converts them to HTML web pages. Then she tries viewing them.

While the pages look great, they download very, very slowly. Even worse, on an average computer, the navigation buttons and calls to action are lost offscreen.

What happened? Morgan forgot about rule 1 — she ignored what she already knew about her audiences, and designed *at* them. Luckily, she hasn't gotten too far into the process, and she can make changes without much trouble.

So she revisits her personas. Here's a refresher:

CONSUMERS want to learn more about the bike, get specifications, contact Morgan and maybe find out how to order. They'll likely learn about the bike either through word of mouth or on the internet.

SHOP OWNERS also want to learn about the bike and get specifications, and then they want to learn more about selling the Road Special.

While both audiences may want to see pictures, they'll consider text specifications and store locations as very important. Her slow-loading home page is a major obstacle, as is the fact that, on a computer with an average video card and monitor, the navigation is actually off the screen.

Morgan tries to create a better design, but she's too close to her own product. She's stumped. So she decides to bring in some outside help; she hires a web designer. They sit down and talk over the personas and goals she mapped out. The designer gets to work, and produces a new look.

This site still features the Road Special, and the photo is more than adequate to bring out the details of the bike. But now the navigation is where folks will expect it. There's some relevant text on the home page, as well. That text is important once folks decide to learn more, and it provides an entry point for search engines, too. (More about that in the chapter on bragging modestly.) Most importantly, the page loads far, far faster — if you only have 15 to 20 seconds to grab someone's attention, the last thing you want is a home page that takes 30 seconds to load.

The new design is clearly for Morgan's two distinct audiences. She's talking *to* them, not *at* them, and she's dressed appropriately.

Visual Design Matters, First

How your web site looks is important. In those crucial first seconds after visitors arrive at your home page, they'll want to see something that appeals to them.

Once you've generated that appeal and dressed appropriately, though, you have to sound smart. So on to the next step.

Sound Smart: Avoiding Conversation Stoppers 5

When you hear an entertaining speaker, or have a conversation with someone who holds your attention, what is it that keeps you listening?

Probably a few things:

- He speaks clearly. You can understand what he's saying. On the internet, that means good *architecture*, and good *code*.
- If he spills his drink on you, he says he's sorry. When those inevitable gaffes happen, you apologize, fix the problem, and move on. On the internet, that's a totally neglected discipline known as *contingency design*.
- He has something interesting to say. You want to hear what he's saying. On the internet that's the same as anywhere else: *content*, and nothing but the content.
- Conversation Marketing requires good architecture, good code, contingency design, and good content. They keep the conversation going, keep it entertaining, and steer folks back on track if their attention wanders.

Architecture: When and Where You Say It

Conversations have a certain flow. And that flow isn't necessarily linear. Sure, you say hello, talk a bit, and then eventually say goodbye, but in between a discussion can meander down a lot of different paths.

If you tried to sketch out a conversation between two people at a networking event, it might look like this:

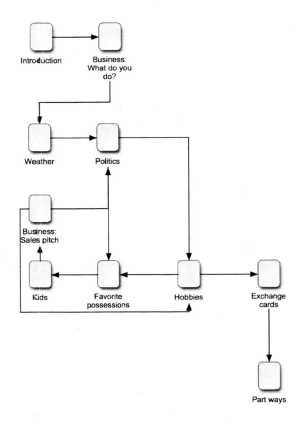

People tend to jump from one subject to the next, but they always have a goal in mind. If you're at a networking event, let's face it: you're there to make good business contacts. You know that you want to meet potential clients and vendors, and exchange cards. But how you get from an introduction to a business card is likely to be different every time.

A web site must treat content the same way. It may all be "static" information on a page, but visitors will move from the home page to their goal (which may change) in many different ways. Great web sites include great *information architecture*. To me, that's the practice of providing clean, useful, practical routes between nuggets of information, where those routes anticipate common lines of inquiry.

I always assume there are a few basic types of users. *Browsers* want to click through a site, finding what they need by using buttons and doing as little typing as possible. *Searchers* want to get to your site, type in a phrase, and go directly to the page they need (or start on Google and do the same thing). *Navigators* want to see a site map or other high-level view of your site, find the area that's relevant, and go there.

Your site needs to cater to all three audiences without playing favorites. That's the other side of good information architecture: structuring content so that your audience gets to pick their own route through it, while at the same time content subtly steers *them* so that the right parts of your message receive emphasis.

I can't give you any great rules for information architecture — it's as much art as it is science — but here are a few guidelines:

- Put the more important stuff at the top of a page, and the fewest clicks away from your home page.
- Try to provide connections between pages on your site with as few clicks as possible.
- Try to keep the number of links on a page to a minimum. More links may seem great, at first, but it can get confusing.
- Remember that everyone browses, searches, and navigates a little differently.

When I put on my architect's hat, I work using a site map — it's a flowchart-style outline of how I'll organize site content, and it serves as a clear picture of the possible conversations I can have with my site visitors.

In other words, information architecture means making sure everyone can find the stuff they want, with a minimum of fuss. It means clarity.

Morgan's Bikes: Creating a Site Map

Just before Morgan creates the design for her site, she starts pondering architecture.

Morgan knows the basic information she wants to communicate, and she knows what her calls to action are (see how important that initial work on personas was?), so she creates her site map:

> *Information architecture and visual design go hand in hand. Where you put stuff on the page provides emphasis and a sense of organization that necessarily back up the architecture. I usually do architecture during the initial design phase, so that I can make sure the two work together. It's a little out of order here — I'd usually do the site map first, then the visual design. But it makes more sense to have it here in the context of this book.*

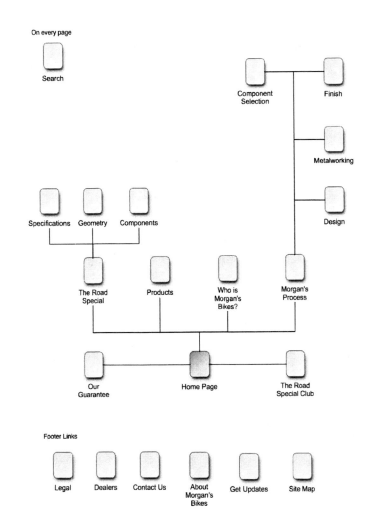

This map works. It's structured well, so that visitors can immediately learn about her main product — the Road Special — and wander through the site to learn more about her company as well.

Note that she's provided a link to Products and another directly to the Road Special, from the home page. Right now the Road Special is her only product. It makes sense to minimize the number of clicks required to get there and to keep options open for the day that Morgan's Bikes has a whole line of products.

The footer links are links available from every page on the site — they may not be in the footer, but that's my personal notation for secondary links that should nevertheless be universally available. They answer questions that may come up at any time in the conversation, just as someone might ask you for your card at any time during that networking event.

You can get from any one page on Morgan's site to any other page in just a few clicks. So this site map accomplishes some important goals.

- It makes all nuggets of information available from all other nuggets, with a minimum of fuss.
- It caters to browsers, searchers, and navigators with clean navigation, a search function, and a site map.
- It still emphasizes certain things — the Road Special and dealers — with unique, top-level links to each of those resources.
- It structures information in a way that will make sense to the audience. (Morgan might want, right on the home page, to talk about the specific metals she uses. That's important to her. But her average customer first wants a higher-level view.)

Note that most site maps will be far, far more complex. Here I've kept most site pages out of it, for the sake of your eyesight.

This site map is a great foundation for Conversation Marketing. It doesn't force anyone into a particular conversation.

Instead, it enables visitors to follow their own path through the information, but offers just enough guidance to make sure they don't get lost.

With a complete design and information architecture, it's time to start building the site. Which brings us to the next step.

Code: How You Say It

Imagine talking to someone who has great ideas but just can't get them across. You can almost feel the brilliance, but you can't get at it because of the background noise. It's frustrating, right? On the internet, good code is part of how you build a good conversation. If your site isn't properly coded, it may not look right, and your conversations will be short.

Visit any web site. Then, if you're using Internet Explorer, click View > Source. See all of that gobbledygook? That's the HTML code that makes the page look the way it does.

HTML (HyperText Markup Language) is a language of structure. It lets a web page designer organize content into paragraphs, tables, and the like. It also includes several ways to control how stuff *looks* — you can control the font, color, and size of text, place images on a page, and do a whole bunch of other prettifying.

People have been trying to improve HTML since the advent of the World Wide Web. It's a very imperfect language, particularly when you're trying to make a really attractive, usable web site. For example, HTML forces designers to use tables — originally meant for the presentation of tabular information — as a layout tool. It also often forces designers to use pictures of text, rather than real, cut-and-pasteable text. It's easy, then, to build a web page that looks OK in many web browsers, but has a terrible, sagging foundation of messy, noncompliant code.

Very few web sites I visit are built on good code. Many print design or web design professionals who are building web sites often cut corners by using a visual layout tool (think Microsoft

FrontPage or Macromedia Dreamweaver). After all, no one *sees* the code. As long as the web page looks OK, who cares?

You should care. Bad code is a conversation ender that creates a whole host of problems. A web site built on bad code:

- May display incorrectly in some web browsers.
- May display incorrectly in more and more browsers as programmers put more effort into creating standards-compliant web browsers.
- Stops search engines in their tracks, preventing good search-engine rankings.
- Violates federal rules for accessibility. This can expose your organization to liability.
- Loads slowly, no matter what you do to reduce the number or size of images on each page.
- Requires additional bandwidth and increases hosting costs.
- Makes maintenance a nightmare.
- Generally gives potential customers the impression that you are not a good resource, thereby ending conversations as fast as a deafening stereo.

It's as though you've faked knowledge on a topic. Sure, you can probably scrimp on your homework and get away with it for a while, but eventually someone who knows the subject is going to find you out. It's tough to recover from that kind of gaffe, right? The same is true if someone visits your web site and it appears broken. Even worse, what if a search engine visits your home page but finds what appears to be an attempt to "cheat" by tricking the search engine into awarding a higher ranking (see chapter 7, "Brag Modestly")? It might be an honest coding error, but many engines will ban sites attempting to game the system. No recovery.

Think of good code as a solid foundation. Use it, and everything you build afterward will be easier. A web site built on clean code:

- Displays consistently in most web browsers.
- Will continue to do so as browsers are upgraded.
- Provides search engines with easy, fast access to all site content, without cheating.
- Adheres to federal accessibility guidelines.
- Loads and renders quickly.
- Saves you money by minimizing bandwidth and hosting costs.
- Is very easy to maintain and build upon.

No one notices good code, just like no one notices if you speak clearly. Good code means good Conversation Marketing because you don't sound silly, and as a result, you sound smart.

"Good" Code, Defined

At the time of this writing, "good" code has the following attributes:

- It separates structure, content, and formatting as much as possible.
- It requires as few lines of code as possible.
- It is standards-compliant.

The easiest way to accomplish good code is by using a combination of HTML, XHTML (Extended HyperText Markup Language) and CSS2 (Cascading Style Sheets, version 2).

I'm not going to provide a lesson in XHTML hybrid programming here. If you want to learn it, check out *Designing with Web Standards*, by Jeffrey Zeldman. It's a fantastic book, written in plain language.

Chances are, though, if you're reading this book you are someone who's going to hire a web designer, or supervise one, who will then build your site. So how do you make sure that the code they're writing is good?

It's not that hard. Here's a checklist of dos and don'ts that you can use to ensure your site is built on solid ground.

- **Do use cascading style sheets.** Ask your web designer about this. If they give you a blank look or say they won't use them, fire them and find another. Repeat as necessary.
- **Do separate style from structure.** Your HTML page should manage structure by defining paragraphs, heading levels, bullets, and the like. It can even do some rudimentary formatting using tables. But font styles, colors, line height, and everything else should be managed in a cascading style sheet.
- **Do make sure your site works in most browsers.** Install Mozilla Firefox (you can find it on Google) and a recent (6.0 or later) Netscape on your computer. Mozilla, in particular, is a stickler for web standards. Test your web site. Your site doesn't have to look 100 percent the same in all browsers, but it should be close. If the page you're viewing looks broken in some browsers and fine in others, it needs to be fixed.
- **Don't do every page differently.** If your web site uses one basic layout throughout, you should be able to use the same code throughout, too. View the source code of two different pages. Take a quick glance: do they appear to be structured about the same? You don't have to know HTML to check this. Just see if the same gibberish shows up, in about the same places, for the first 20 to 30 lines of the source code. If it does not, again, talk to your designer and find out why.

No examples in this chapter. What do I look like, an HTML professor? But if you want to learn a lot more about standards-based HTML coding, buy, borrow, or steal a copy of Jeffrey Zeldman's *Designing with Web Standards*.

Contingency Design: Saying You're Sorry

Ever had a miserable customer experience, but walked away smiling? The lousy dinner that was followed up with free dessert? The terrible phone service that was compensated by two months free? How about a free first-class upgrade after your flight was delayed?

Why did you walk away happy? The meal sucked. The phone company drove you nuts. And you got to your destination nine hours late, after eating lousy airport food. You walked away happy because someone said, "We're very sorry, and here's how we're going to make up for it." They expressed concern, and yeah, they bribed you.

You can do the same thing on your web site, through a technique called *contingency design* — the Zen art of admitting things will go wrong and figuring out how to apologize, in advance. Contingency design is essential if you want to sound smart. Because no web interaction can be perfect, and it's up to you to help your audience walk away smiling.

Morgan's Bikes: Contingency Design

PAGE NOT FOUND. Morgan now has a web guru working on building her site. Problem is, the new site is going to replace an existing one. Folks may have bookmarked pages on the old site, or they may follow outdated links to her site from other web sites or search engines. If a potential customer does that, what will they see?

Well, if her web developer failed to practice good contingency design, they see an ugly, generic 404 Page Not Found message that begs them to go away and never come back. That conversation didn't even get started.

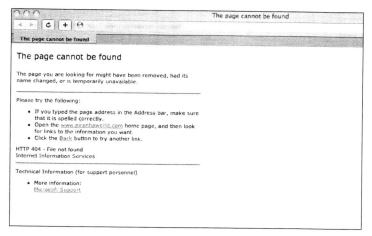

A bad "page not found" error. Not very informative, is it?

If, on the other hand, Morgan's web pro engages in just a little contingency design, they might see a nicely designed, useful page. Here's how my company's site deals with the problem.

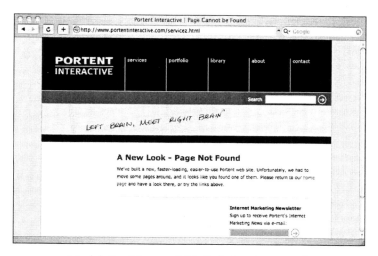

Much better. The user didn't find what they wanted, but at least they're not lost.

This error page provides navigation, clear indication that you're in the right place, and instructions on what to do next. The conversation continues.

WHERE THE HECK IS...? A visitor to Morgan's site uses its onsite search tool to find "wheels." But she types in "weels" — maybe she had too much coffee. Bad contingency design yields a "Sorry, no results found" and relies on the visitor to figure out what happened. Good contingency design shows a page that says something like "We didn't find anything for 'weels,' but we did find results for related terms. Here are the top 10 results." All fixed.

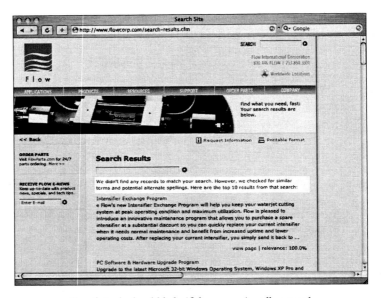

Search tools should help if the user misspells a word.

So a little forethought helps the visitor find her way past those inevitable little mishaps, and respects her interest in your message.

Good contingency design means always having to say you're sorry, but never having to say "See you later." If you want to learn more about contingency design, check out *Defensive Design for the Web*, by 37signals (Matthew Linderman and John Fried). It's a definitive work on the subject.

Content: The 800-pound Gorilla

All of my chattering on about code, architecture, and contingency design may make you think that content — that stuff people actually *see* — isn't important. Not true.

I've spent most of this chapter talking about how your web campaign will speak. But what it says is more than half the battle.

Written content must be crafted to speak to your audience; go back and look at your list of personas, and make sure that your text content really works for the lowest common denominator in that group.

Images, streaming video, and any other content on your site has to be accessible to that audience, too. If your audience is using dial-up internet and six-year-old computers, sending them streaming video probably makes no sense. And the content of those images and rich media content matter, as well — one visitor's entertainment is another's insult. Always consider the mores and quirks of your audience.

Now you're saying, "Four paragraphs? That's *it*?"

Yes. That's it. Because well-crafted content is a subjective, subtle, tricky business. Trickier even than design. If you want to succeed, and you're not comfortable producing your own content, get a pro. But here are a few basic rules of online content.

- Try to have no more than 250 words on a page. If you have more text than that, break it into multiple pages.
- Use headings to divide your page into digestible chunks.
- Write simply, whenever possible. The web is *not* a good place to hit the thesaurus. It's harder to read text on a screen than on paper.
- If you're using photographs, compress them as much as you can without reducing quality.
- Most of the time, compress photographs using JPG compression.

- Most of the time, compress line art using GIF compression.
- Use a photo editing program like Adobe Photoshop, JASC Paint Shop Pro or Macromedia Fireworks to resize your photos *before* you place them on the page.
- Don't use video or audio unless you have a really good reason.
- Remember, everything on the page should have a purpose!

A good conversation gets to the point and holds everyone's attention. Conversation Marketing does all that, and more. Sound smart and you'll have more internet conversations and more customers.

Sound Smart: Making Sense of It All

This was a long, challenging chapter. The good news is, you made it! The bad news is, you'll have to read it again and again, and read the other materials I've referenced, and spend a few hours per day researching the latest developments, if you want to consistently produce good content, organize it effectively, and then deliver it using a site that's based on web standards and good contingency design.

If you're a web pro, or want to become one, that's exactly what you should do. Become a student. Live and breath this stuff. It pays off.

Happily, if you're not interested in becoming a web professional, you don't have to do that. Use this chapter as your guide when you plan, supervise, and then evaluate the professionals you hire. This chapter is a great yardstick with which to measure those who do the work for you.

Make a Connection: Continuing the Conversation

6

If you're networking, enduring those long, uncomfortable silences while attempting to bridge the gulf between little knots of conversations, and then you finally get into a chat with someone who's a great potential client, what do you do next? Something like this?

YOU: ...so that's what my company does. It really seems that we could do some great work together.
POTENTIAL CLIENT: You're right. I'd like to talk more.
YOU: [*silence as you walk off into the crowd*]

Or this...?

YOU: ...so that's what my company does. It really seems that we could do some great work together.
POTENTIAL CLIENT: You're right. I'd like to talk more.
YOU: Great, here's my card.
You take a card out of your pocket and hold it out to the potential client. They reach for it...
YOU: Oh, psych!
...and you snatch it away at the last second.
POTENTIAL CLIENT: Ha ha. OK, give me the card please.
YOU: OK, here you go... nope, changed my mind! Hahahaha....

Doesn't make sense, does it? Well, at least 90 percent of the web sites out there do one of these two things. Folks invest time, money, and effort to build a site that will grab the attention of a visitor. Then they invest even more time and money to get visitors to their site, in pay-per-click ads, search-engine optimization, and who knows what else. Then they do the online equivalent of walking away.

You've made a pretty substantial investment of time, money, and energy to get folks to your web site. They've come, they like what they see, and they want to ponder a bit. Now you have two choices:

- Hope they bookmark your site, or at least remember the web address, and come back when they want more information.
- Politely ask them if they'd like you to keep in touch.

The former is great if your company name is, say, Nike or CNN. But it won't do you much good if you're Morgan's Bikes, or even ModernBride.com. Some will remember you and return, but there's a chunk of that audience that wants to learn more, to be reminded of your existence, and to know when there's important news.

That's where the latter choice — politely asking — comes in handy. Think about a big networking event — you've gone through the group-to-group trolling and all the awkwardness that's entailed. Now you're talking to someone who's very interested in your product. When ready to move on, what do you do? You ask her for her business card, and ask if you can call her in the next week or so. You've made a connection, and in so doing you've increased the odds that you can continue the conversation.

On the web, the most common way to make a connection is e-mail. It's ubiquitous, everyone knows how to use it, and it doesn't depend on others coming to find you. But there are other methods that are worth remembering, too: RSS and its close relative, Podcasting.

E-mail: Powerful, but Dangerous

If I say "e-mail marketing," what's the first word that pops into your head? Spam?

Thought so.

But not all e-mail marketing is spam. There is a right way to draw subscribers to an e-mail newsletter, and actually have them feel good when you send them something.

How can you use e-mail as a marketing tool, and not get tagged as a spammer? First of all, keep in mind that there are two definitions of spam: the legal definition, with which it's pretty easy to comply, and the emotional definition. It's the emotional definition you have to watch out for — folks are quick to use the s-word (*spam*, not that other one) for any and all e-mail that they feel is either unsolicited, inappropriate, or otherwise naughty. It's very easy to run afoul of the emotional definition, so stick to these rules:

OPT-IN ONLY

Only send e-mail to those who expressly ask for it. Put a simple form on your web site — all you really need is the subscriber's e-mail address, remember — and only send e-mail to those who complete that form.

There is one, and only one, exception to this rule. If you have an existing customer list, and want to sign up those people for another list, send them a polite e-mail inviting them to subscribe. Do not sign them up and ask them to unsubscribe! That's just rude, like eating the last piece of cake and then asking if anyone wants it.

An opt-in-only list will start smaller, it's true. But a small list is a targeted one — your subscribers will truly appreciate receiving your e-mails.

KEEP IT SMALL

Your e-mail message should be no larger than 15 kilobytes. The total file size for all images and text should never be larger than this number. If you're not sure what I'm talking about here, hire someone who understands e-mail template design. Believe me, it's worth it.

There's another definition of spam, the automated one. Most companies use automatic spam filters now — it's very easy to send out an e-mail that trips their alarms. When that happens, your intended recipient may not even see it. Follow these rules, though, and you'll minimize the chances of getting the spam filter smackdown.

Remember that all your e-mail has to do is get the reader to click through to your web site. You don't have to show your product in an extra-large photo, or provide ten paragraphs explaining your service. Save that for your site. Keep the message compact, and don't use more than one or two images in your message. The result will be a small, fast-loading e-mail message.

Try to design an e-mail message that looks good in a standard Microsoft Outlook or Eudora preview pane. At a minimum, someone viewing your message in a small window should see your logo and the basic message.

Stay away from fancy technologies in your e-mail. Restrict yourself to HTML and images, or even better, plain text. Macromedia Flash and other streaming technologies seem like great e-mail gadgets, but they're disastrous: they lead to bloated messages and a whole array of compatibility issues. Don't drive your audience crazy — keep the streaming stuff on your web site, and out of the e-mail.

Avoid the One-Image Gag

Even an HTML e-mail must include some text. Don't send an e-mail that's just one big image. Most spam filters now check for e-mails that contain images and no text, and automatically assign them to the junk heap.

Be Honest

Your e-mail subject line should clearly describe the content of the message. And the e-mail's reply-to address should be an address that goes to a human being.

Finally, make sure there is a clear Unsubscribe link in your message.

Follow Your Instincts

Lastly, follow your gut. Would the e-mail you're about to send annoy you? Will it feel like someone on a sidewalk pushing fliers in people's faces? If so, reconsider. Chances are you don't engage in a conversation with someone, or hand them a business card, unless there's a reason. Conversation Marketing through e-mail should follow the same rule.

RSS and Podcasting: Emerging Options

RSS, also known as "really simple syndication," lets folks subscribe directly to a feed that delivers updated headings and new site pages. I'm not going to get into the technical details. Trust me — it's not that difficult. There are a few great sites where you can learn how to create an RSS feed; do a quick search on the web and you'll find what you need.

The beauty of RSS is that you can use any one of a number of feed readers (some are free) to aggregate lots of feeds from lots of different web sites. And the presence of RSS is growing — Apple's latest version of Safari has built-in RSS support. So does Mozilla Firefox.

If you maintain an RSS feed and visitors subscribe to it, they'll see any new information every time they open their feed reader.

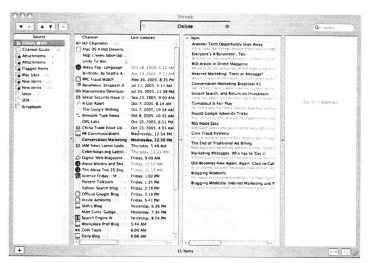

This is my favorite Mac OS X newsreader, Shrook, in action. It shows all of the RSS feeds to which I subscribe, in one place. I can quickly see what's new, and scan the headlines to see if there's anything interesting.

Although the geeks love RSS, it hasn't caught on with the masses yet. But it will. If you have a technically advanced audience, or just want to get ahead of the curve, think about including an RSS feed in your site. It takes very little time and provides one more way to keep in touch.

RSS is one more invitation to converse. It lets people sidle over, listen for a moment, and decide if they want to join in. As such, it's a great Conversation Marketing tool when you have an audience that may not want to give you any information just yet.

PODCASTING: THE YOUNGER BROTHER OF RSS

Chances are you've heard the word podcast. It seems mysterious, but the concept is pretty simple: a podcast is an RSS feed that includes some form of audio or video content. Think of it as TiVo for radio or for online video.

Subscribers to a podcast with a compatible RSS reader are automatically updated as new audio or video is posted to the feed. Most folks then transfer the audio or video to their MP3 player (hence the term *podcast*; iPods rule the world right now).

Again, I won't go into details — suffice it to say that if your business involves any form of public speaking, music, or other things that are best communicated via audio or video, you need to consider podcasting. It offers the same advantages as RSS, and is a great way to converse with your audience if they're short on time, because they can download the conversation and literally take it with them.

Morgan's Bikes: Connecting Here, There, and Everywhere

When we last left Morgan, she was making progress. She has a site design, a good, well-coded set of pages, and content. She's invested a fair chunk of her money and time, and her site's now live. Sales aren't bad. A $6,000 bicycle is not a casual purchase, and Morgan knows that her best customers get to know her company before they buy, either through a local dealer or directly.

She'd hoped to get more calls and ongoing conversations going from her web site, but it hasn't happened yet.

So, she starts the *RoadTrip*, a biweekly newsletter. In it, she gives training tips, maintenance advice, and news about her company. Occasionally she reviews other products.

She lets visitors sign up for the newsletter from her site. She also sends a sign-up invitation to all customers who have given her e-mail addresses in the past.

She immediately gets a handful of sign-ups, resulting in a list of about 200 people who want to keep in touch. Some of them start sending her inquiries after receiving a newsletter. Within a few months, two list subscribers have become customers. Why? They liked her, and her newsletters — in a world where there are dozens of custom-bike manufacturers, building that relationship can make all the difference.

I said she sends an invitation. She does not just sign them all up. She's being polite.

Keep in Touch

However you decide to keep the conversation going — e-mail, RSS, or something else — make sure you live up to expectations. Send subscribers an e-mail when you have important news. Update your RSS feed regularly. Record some new audio and post it to your podcast feed. Remember, these people said "Yes, please talk to me!" If you do that, there's a better chance you can stay "front of mind" and a much better chance you'll turn a visitor into a customer.

You can also draw people to your web site by bragging (modestly). That's the next chapter.

Brag Modestly: Polite Conversation Starters

Here are two scenarios. You tell me which is better:

A writer you know goes to your weekly breakfast networking meeting — you know, those excruciating card-swapping exercises that usually include stale bagels and crappy coffee. She walks around, shaking hands with people, intruding into conversations and stating that she's the best writer in town, and they'd be stupid not to hire her.

OK, now it's the same breakfast meeting, same stale bagels, same writer friend, but change the scenario a bit. This time she sticks with you as you move from conversation to conversation, and you introduce her to a few people you know as "That writer I told you about — you could *really* use her services."

The first scenario won't really benefit her, right? In fact, her behavior reflects poorly on you. In the second scenario, though, she looks much better, and it's likely that someone there will want to start working with her.

What's the difference? In the second case, she let someone else brag for her — you could say that she bragged *modestly*, by letting you recommend her.

The same method works well on the internet. The breakfast networking meeting is typically going to be a search engine, and you brag modestly by achieving a high natural ranking or by creating a well-composed pay-per-click ad. You can start a lot of conversations through search engines.

Why Search Engines?

There are, of course, other ways to get people to visit your web site: banners, e-mail marketing, and word of mouth all work. But well over 80 percent of internet users visit a search engine

I'm not saying ignore stuff like banner ads. But given a limited budget, you have to pick your venues. A search engine is clearly the place to start.

to find what they want online. Eighty percent is probably a pretty modest estimate, actually. When's the last time you found anything online without visiting Google, or Yahoo, or MSN?

Love 'em, hate 'em, search engines are a marketing fact of life if you're trying to grow your business using the internet.

There are vast, bubbling vats of snake oil out there, and salesmen trying to convince you that theirs is the One True Way to achieve a high natural ranking in the search engines. The trick is avoiding the hooey and using a strategy that works. For me, that's always been a balance of pay-per-click advertising and natural rankings.

A Quick Search-Engine Anatomy Lesson: PPC and Natural Rankings

Everyone knows, I think, what a search engine does: You type in a keyword or phrase, like "chocolate candy," and you get a list of results, ranked by relevance. Click on a result and you land on that web site.

What you may not know is that search engines typically deliver two sets of results: free, or natural, results and sponsored, or pay-per-click (PPC), results.

On Google, for example, the natural search results are displayed in the big column on the left. The PPC results are at the very top and in the small column on the right:

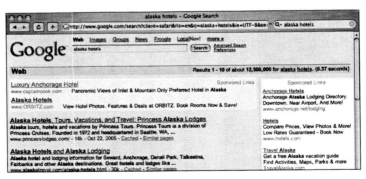

On Google, PPC results are on right-hand side of the page, and sometimes on top.

What's the difference? Search engines determine natural results by applying formulae that they develop — the results can't be influenced through payments or sponsorship.

PPC results are paid for by the advertisers, who bid for the best ranking on a keyword-by-keyword basis. The highest bidder gets the #1 spot, the second highest the #2 spot, and so on. Some engines, like Google, tweak these sponsored results a bit according to keyword relevance of the ad and clickthru performance. I won't go into that here. If you want to learn the finer points of PPC algorithms, well, maybe wait for my next book.

Natural search results are where the long-term money is. The vast majority of users (75 percent or more) look at the top 5 to 10 natural results, and that's it. But getting a high natural ranking takes time, and a lot of effort, and sometimes a lot of writers. Imagine trying to get the #1 spot for a phrase like "Alaska hotels" — type it into Google and see how many results there are. Right now, I see over 11 million. Get a top-5 spot, and you're set. Get on the second page, and your work's for nothing.

PPC results only grab about 15 percent of the audience, but you can get a top rank in a few minutes — it's all about how much you want to bid.

A balanced campaign, then, will combine smart PPC with a long-term focus on natural results. The PPC ads quickly generate income. The natural rankings may eventually do a lot more, if you can achieve a high enough position.

Which Words and Phrases?

Keywords are the crux of a search engine campaign — pick the right ones and you can set up PPC ads and pursue natural rankings that will select and deliver useful traffic. Pick the wrong ones and end up accumulating, instead — even a #1 rank may not generate useful results for you. In other words, keywords ensure you enter into the right conversations, with the right people.

Put careful thought into the phrases you pick. In Google AdWords and Yahoo Sponsored Search, you can use their keyword suggestion tools to find the best phrases. Tools like WordTracker can help, as well. Just use common sense.

Say you pick a phrase like "SSH client" — trust me, it's a big one. Folks typing in this term might be searching for a free SSH client, like OpenSSH. Or they might be looking for a purchased product, like F-Secure. Bidding for the top rank for this term may mean you have to compete for ranking across a very broad subject area. It's inefficient and may lead to a very poor return on investment.

It's like driving for an hour to go to a realtor networking event when you build kites. Sure, you might find a realtor who happens to be looking for a kite, but chances are you're entering the wrong conversation.

PPC Guidelines

Three simple rules for PPC campaigns:

DON'T BID TOO MUCH. Keep your bids under control. (See "The Cost of Conversion: Return on Investment," page 77.) If you spend $3 per click, $3,000 a month, for five sales that only generate $1,500 in income, you're probably killing yourself.

WRITE GOOD COPY. Pay attention to your ad copy. There's an art form to writing a truly effective PPC ad. It may not be as important as the bid management, but it matters. Have a clear call to action, and make sure your ad clearly states what you offer.

DEEP LINK. Don't just link to your home page — each PPC ad should link directly to the product or service or subject most relevant to the ad. It should link to the page that'll generate a conversion (a sale, a sign-up, a registration, etc.) for you.

And the most important rule: **TREAT EVERY PAGE ON YOUR SITE AS A HOME PAGE.** If folks are going to be deep-linking into your site, the page they land on has to make sense, offer a clear call to action, and help move them along in the conversation. It's as if someone walks up in the middle of your chat with another person. If he understands what you're saying, he may join in. If it makes no sense to him, he walks away.

Natural Search Guidelines

Getting a good natural-search ranking is like having a major newspaper write about you. The next time you show up at a networking event, everyone will want to converse. Online, a top ranking can deliver an endless supply of potential customers, which supplies any Conversation Marketing campaign with an ongoing, interested audience.

However, effective natural-search marketing can be very, very tricky. To stay sane, think about what a search engine's job is: deliver the most relevant content to users. Make it easy for search engines to measure your relevance. Focus on good architecture, good content, and good code. And follow a few basics:

UPDATE YOUR SITE. Add new stuff to your site, all the time. Search engines award higher relevance to sites that are more active and have fresher content. You should keep your site up-to-date, anyway, as you observe and adjust — this is just one more reason. People won't talk to you more than twice if you say the exact same thing both times, right?

KEEP THE IMPORTANT STUFF ON TOP. Search engines respect structure, so put the most important stuff as few clicks as possible from your home page. That'll ensure that the search engines rate you by what *you feel* is most valuable. Good structure is good for visitors, too. See chapter 5, "Sound Smart: Avoiding Conversation Stoppers."

TAG EVERYTHING. Make sure every page has a relevant title, description, and keyword tag. And make sure every image and link has proper ALT and TITLE attributes, too. If you don't know what this means, hire someone who does.

Remember, though, this is a *long-term* strategy — it takes some sellers up to a year to see positive changes in their search results. So always seek a balance between PPC and natural search results.

There are dozens of little things you can do to maximize natural search results. What you really need to do is hire a professional. Ahem.

Search-Marketing Firms: Three Signs You Shouldn't Hire Someone

There are lots of reputable search-marketers out there. Heck, I'm one of them. But there are a lot of folks who are either totally ignorant or outright swindlers. If you hear these phrases, run, get in your car, lock the doors, and find another firm:

"We guarantee a top-10 listing!" My blood boils every time I hear that. No one can guarantee a top-10 natural ranking for a specific term. Search engines change their rules all the time, and you're generally competing with thousands or millions of other pages. No one has a special relationship with the search engines either.

"We'll submit you to 10,000 search engines!" Uh, great, but there aren't 10,000 search engines. Whoever tells you this can't even do math. There are maybe twenty search engines that matter, and of those, three to five really control the market: Google, Yahoo, MSN, Ask Jeeves, and Dogpile, in that order.

"We'll get you 500 links right away." Gaaaah! Run! This firm will engage in a practice called "link farming." I won't go into details, but trust me — the results are not good.

Generally, trust your instincts. If marketers seem smarmy, they probably are. If you feel dirty every time you leave their office, you probably don't want them working on your search marketing campaign, either.

Bad search-marketing will deliver a lot of long, uncomfortable silences to the conversation. Good search-marketing will keep a vibrant chat going for as long as you want it.

Other Modest Brags

There are a lot of other ways to brag modestly.

- **BLOGGING** can provide an opportunity to teach your audience about what you do, without a sales pitch.
- **NEWSLETTER SPONSORSHIP** can let you support an e-mail newsletter about a relevant topic and get some publicity, too.

- Even **BANNER ADS** can be modest, depending on how you do them.
- Sending out a **PRESS RELEASE** using one of the web-based wire services can generate great buzz and get you some additional search benefits, too.

You can supplement any campaign using these methods. Just remember, though, that the search engine is still king on the internet — any effective marketing strategy must take that into account.

Regardless of how you do it, understand that bragging modestly is not an option. It's a requirement. The internet is packed with people shouting and waving their wares to every passer-by. If you can take a moderate tone and pick the right audience, you'll stand out.

Morgan's Bikes: Morgan Gets Modest

Morgan's new site is skillfully coded and structured. She starts adding her newsletters to the site, too, so there's steady content growth. But her marketing team told her it'd be at least a few months before she starts showing up in natural search, so she starts a pay-per-click campaign.

She uses AdWords and Yahoo Search Marketing (formerly Overture), and bids on the terms "custom road bicycles" and "custom bikes." Results aren't bad, but she finds she's spending a *lot* of money on the "custom bikes" advertisement, and doesn't seem to be getting results. After a little research, her marketing team figures out why — "bikes" can mean a motorcycle or a bicycle. She's in a very unfocused search area when she bids on that term. She changes her phrase to "custom bicycles" and gets higher clickthru and conversion rates.

Encouraged, Morgan has her team write a press release about a new Road Special she's introducing. They send it out using PRWeb (www.prweb.com), which is inexpensive and highly optimized for web visibility. As a result, she shows up #1 in Google and Yahoo news searches for the terms "bicycles" and "custom bicycles" for a day or two, and anyone who subscribes to news alerts for those terms learns about her company. Traffic jumps, and a few magazines even call her for a brief statement so they can mention her in their next issues.

Modest bragging worked well: she generated direct traffic through PPC and got some attention in both online and offline media.

Now it's time to figure out if any of this is leading to better sales, by observing and adjusting.

Observe and Adjust: Keeping the Conversation Going

8

So, you've finished your site. It's launched, it looks great, and you're ready to start taking orders, or getting the word out, or doing whatever it is that your internet-communications campaign is supposed to do. All done, right? Nope. The conversation's just getting started.

What makes a good conversation? If all participants have something to talk about, and they're polite, intelligent communicators, what keeps things going? The give-and-take. If you are at a party, chatting with someone, you're constantly observing his response to what you say and do, and adjusting the conversation accordingly. You do this pretty much unconsciously.

You can do almost the same thing on your web site. By tracking a few basics, you can gather information about your audience's response to your campaign, and adjust accordingly. Trust me: Your audience will love you for it because you'll provide a more relevant conversation that feels as though it's directed right at them. Nothing keeps you in a conversation like knowing it's just for you.

You can observe without intruding. Every example and principle outlined in this chapter is completely anonymous, and won't violate the privacy of those visiting your site.

The Basics: Web Traffic Analysis

Let's start with the simple stuff. You can always measure how many folks visit your site, which pages they like the most (and least), where they come from, and how often they return.

No matter how you set up your web site, it'll be stored on a web server. That server answers requests from visitors' web browsers and delivers pages to them. And every request is logged in a file.

If you opened that log file in a word processor, it'd be pretty hard to read. Impossible, actually, unless you have a lot of spare time on your hands. Fortunately, there's a whole category of software out there called *web traffic analyzers*. Some are free, some are outrageously expensive, but all will take the babbling randomness of your traffic logs and turn it into a sensible, readable report. Chances are you already have a tool like this at your disposal. If not, keep reading — I have a few recommendations at the end of this section.

Once you have access to your web traffic report, there are five statistics to focus on.

HITS. A *hit* is one download of one file from your web site. So, if your home page consists of three images, a style sheet (style .css, for example), and the page itself (let's say index.html), then every time a browser downloads that page, five hits are recorded. On some sites, a single downloaded page can account for dozens of hits. Hits are a good measure of overall server usage, but while it may sound impressive to say, "My site got 10,000 hits this month," hits don't tell you much about site traffic.

SESSIONS. A *session* is one browser visiting your site, one time. So, if I come to your site ten times in one day, that counts for ten sessions. This is a better measure of traffic than a hit, clearly, but there's a problem that I can illustrate with this example: If everyone in your office has your site set as their home page, then every time they start their browser, they generate a new session on your server. Think about it. That means that five or six people can generate a lot of sessions, which doesn't necessarily give you an accurate look at your site's appeal. It's great to have folks come back to your site, but you need to know how many individuals see it, too.

VISITS. That's where *visits* — or more specifically, *unique visits* — come in. A unique visit is one visitor coming to your site any number of times in a given time period. So, if I come to your site 300 times in a month, I'll still only count as a single unique visitor for that month. You need to know how many individuals arrive at your site, because each unique visit starts a conversation, and each conversation is an opportunity. (Note that some reporting tools call a unique visit a *unique session* — it's confusing, I know, but if you see "unique," chances are you're on the right track.)

PAGE VIEWS. A *page view* is one browser downloading one page, one time. Combined with visits, page views can tell you how successful your conversations are. If you have 100 unique visitors a day, and only 100 page views, that's a bad sign — each visitor is only viewing a single page of your site. If, on the other hand, you have 100 unique visitors and 500 page views, that's better — it means that visitors are spending a little time looking around your site. Generally, a high page-view-to-unique-visit ratio is a good thing. Don't get carried away, though — if visitors are viewing a lot of pages per visit, they may be getting lost.

REFERRERS. The most underused statistic, and the most important one, a *referrer* records when a visitor clicks a link taking him from another web site to yours. If a potential customer types "custom road bicycle" into Google, and then clicks a link to MorgansBikes.com, Google will show up in the traffic report as a referrer. Even better, most traffic-analysis tools will also show that the phrase "custom road bicycle" generated traffic to the site. That's valuable intelligence — it tells you what your audience was thinking about when they came looking for you.

Many log analyzers provide other bells and whistles, too: Click paths, least popular pages, exit pages, and entrance pages may all be tallied and tabulated for your viewing pleasure. As you get a feel for web traffic reporting, you can put all of this to good use. But you can learn a lot with the five basics.

Morgan's Bikes: Directing Traffic

Morgan's new site is live! With a clean design and easy access to lots of useful information, the site gets rave reviews. She's receiving lots of e-mail inquiries from shop owners she knows, and from members of her local bicycle club. But she's not getting a lot of love from the vast audience of cyclists who don't already know her. She's not sure why, so she takes a look at her traffic reports for the first month. Here's a quick summary:

HITS	46,234
SESSIONS	3,012
UNIQUE VISITS	210
PAGE VIEWS	1,102
REFERRERS	99% "no referrer"

This sheds some light on the problem. The hit count looks great, but doesn't mean very much. Visits and referrers highlight the issue. She's only had 210 unique visitors in a single month. And 99 percent of her traffic had no referrer — that's a fancy way of saying that 99 percent of her visitors came to her site by typing "morgansbikes.com" into their web browsers. Only *two* visitors found her through a link from another site. In internet marketing terms, she's invisible.

Morgan digs a little deeper and looks at the most popular pages on her site: the top four pages are her home page, then three dealer-information pages. The issue becomes clearer now. The only folks who are finding her are *dealers* (and maybe a few consumers), because they receive her print catalog. No one's finding her in search engines, or from other web links.

Morgan's educated now, but not discouraged. She's learned two valuable facts:

- **THE DEALERS REALLY DO WANT TO USE HER SITE.** With 210 unique visitors, but 3,012 sessions, she knows that visitors come back to her site *a lot* once they visit it — an average of 15 times per month, in fact. So her site's "sticky," at least for dealers.
- **SHE NEEDS TO CONSIDER SOME ONLINE MARKETING,** or something else, to get more consumers to notice her.

She knows why some folks are joining the conversation, and why others aren't. She can use that information to refine her marketing campaign.

Web Traffic Analysis Software

If you're hosting your web site with a web-hosting company, or if you have an IT department at your disposal, you should already have access to a traffic-analysis tool. If you don't, find a new hosting company (or a new IT person!). Analysis tools are easy to find and set up. A few good programs are:

Urchin: My personal favorite. Urchin comes in a few flavors — the basic version isn't very expensive, and provides accurate measurement of sessions, page views, hits, and referring traffic. Upgrades include a campaign-tracking module that lets you track which banners, e-mail messages, search terms, and ads generate the most business for you, and a powerful e-commerce module that ties sales directly to campaigns. Urchin is so good, Google bought them. You can learn more about Urchin at www.urchin.com or www.google.com/analytics.

WebTrends: Now owned by NetIQ, WebTrends is one of the most popular web-log analysis packages. It provides the same toolset as Urchin — preference is based on personal taste. I recommend comparing them if you're going to be buying a log analyzer.

Webalizer: Probably the best free log-analysis tool out there, Webalizer provides the basics. It doesn't do a good job of measuring unique visitors, and the referrer analysis leaves a lot to be desired, but you can't beat the price.

Or, you can hire a full-service internet marketing company and let them worry about the details.

The one thing you *can't* do is ignore your web traffic statistics. Doing so is like talking solely to make noise, or ignoring the other people in the conversation. Conversation Marketing cannot work if you don't observe at least basic traffic statistics.

The Next Step: Knowing What Works — Conversions

Tracking how many folks come to your site, and where they come from, is great. It can provide you with a very basic measure of success. But the real measure of a successful marketing investment is the return — the ability of that campaign to deliver conversions. A conversion happens anytime someone answers your call to action.

Whether you're selling, persuading, discussing, or entertaining, you have an end in mind — a call to action. Remember all of those calls to action in chapter 3? Each call to action is an opportunity to measure how well your internet marketing campaign is performing. Every time a prospective dealer looks for another dealer to contact, views search data, or, even better, contacts Morgan with a question or to request the newsletter, that indicates a level of interest beyond a simple glance through her site.

The next step, then, is measuring four different things:

- How often visitors to your site respond to calls to action.
- Which calls to action they respond to.
- Where they come from (a search engine, an e-mail, a banner) when they respond.
- How much each response is worth, and how much it costs.

That last one can be daunting, but bear with me, and you'll see you can almost always figure it out.

How Often, and Which Call to Action

The first step is measuring how often visitors respond to a specific call to action. Typically, a call to action means someone completes some kind of form, or downloads a file, or takes some other action and then lands on a page on your web site that they wouldn't otherwise see. Here's an example:

If a dealer contacts Morgan using her web site, that dealer fills out a form and clicks Send. They then land on a thank-you page.

That thank-you page is a unique web page that isn't delivered to a web browser unless a dealer has completed the Dealership Opportunities form. So, if her web traffic report shows a page view for that page, Morgan knows that someone has completed this form. Voilà! By using the tools already at her disposal, she knows when someone responds to that specific call to action.

Wait a minute, you say. That's an easy one. What about when someone checks dealer search data? They're not filling out a form, then, are they?

True enough. But again, the only time someone will view the Dealer Searches in My Area page *should* be when he or she is figuring out whether there's enough demand in the area to warrant selling the Road Special. Sure, folks might randomly happen by that page, but if Morgan's site is well designed, consumers should stick to their side of the fence, and the flow of traffic to the Dealer Searches in My Area page should be fairly pure.

OK, fine, you say. But what about dealers who just pick up the phone after seeing the site? That's a valid issue — you never record 100 percent of your conversions. But I always prefer to err toward the conservative, and so treating web conversions as your sole measure of success will play it safe. In a face-to-face conversation, some folks don't let on that they're happy/sad/mad about what you're saying. Some do, though, and it's prudent to watch for those responses. Same thing goes in Conversation Marketing.

THE COST OF CONVERSION: RETURN ON INVESTMENT

Each response to a call to action has a cost for you. Whether you're using a banner ad, or making pay-per-click bids on Google or Yahoo Search Marketing, or hiring an agency to build your web site, you pay money for that potential customer/voter/member/devotee.

How do you quantify the cost of conversion? Sometimes it's easy. Sometimes it's not.

EASY. You're selling a product. Each product sells for $40, retail. It costs you $10 to make, stock, and ship each one. Your web site cost $10,000, and your advertising is another $1,000 per month. Your site sells 80 items in one month. Loosely figured, this comes out to:

$833.33/*month*	your site ($10,000 divided by 12 months)
$1,000.00/*month*	advertising
$1,833.33/*month*	TOTAL for internet marketing
$1,833.33/80 *items*	= $22.92 cost to you per sale

Since you earn $30 per product sold, you're getting by.

LESS EASY. You're collecting leads — either for callbacks to sell a product or to register folks to vote, or for something else. You can't necessarily attach each conversion to a specific profit or value — if you're trying to acquire members or persuade someone, there's not necessarily any intrinsic dollar value. But you *can* compare the cost of conversion on the web to your cost of conversion off the web. This doesn't have to be exact, but here's the gist:

OFFLINE CONVERSIONS: ROAD SPECIAL DEALERS

$6,000/*year*	magazine ad
$6,000/*year*	Interbike visit, hospitality suite, hotel
$1,000/*year*	phone calls to dealers
$13,000/*year*	TOTAL
100 *dealer inquiries in 2004*	$13,000/100 leads = $130/lead
10 *new dealers acquired offline in 2004*	$13,000/10 dealers = $1,300/dealer

Online Conversions

$833.33/month	web site (see above — I'm being lazy)
$100/month	pay-per-click ads
$933.33/month	TOTAL for dealer marketing
10 dealer inquiries in the first month	$933.33/10 inquiries = $93.33/lead
2 dealers acquired online	$933.33/2 dealers = $466.67/dealer

The web's not converting a lot yet, but the cost is lower, so it balances out. If you were measuring conversions and return on investment (ROI) for something that has no final value, you could stop here. But Morgan can take things a step further. She can keep track of where each dealer first contacted her (on- or offline) and see whether dealers contacting her through one medium or the other do a better job of selling her product. Then she can truly measure the return on her internet marketing investment, and adjust her campaign accordingly.

What's Converting?

Finally, you want to know which specific online marketing efforts are generating responses. Are your e-mails garnering more conversions? Or those banner ads you bought on Yahoo?

This is one of the toughest areas of internet marketing. If you're a web geek, you can build a measurement solution of your own that'll track conversions back to individual sources. But there are a lot of pre-built tools out there these days that can do the job for you.

Yahoo Search Marketing has a built-in conversion tracking tool. With a little cutting-and-pasting you can measure whether your pay-per-click campaigns are generating conversions, and the cost.

Google AdWords has their own solution, of course, that lets you measure conversions and ROI for AdWords campaigns. they also have Google Analytics, which is free, but invitation-only at this writing.

Urchin offers a slightly pricey ($3,500) add-on to their standard web traffic analysis package that lets you track conversions and cost per conversion, right down to the search engine and keyword. It also lets you track conversions from banners, links, and other assets.

And, of course, you can always hire an internet marketing agency to not only track conversions but analyze and provide advice based on that data.

Which tool's right for you? If you're on a tight budget and you're carrying out a pay-per-click campaign on Google or Yahoo Search Marketing, stick with their tools. But Urchin, and tools like it, will let you keep a more complete picture of what's driving conversions to your site, because these more complete tools track natural search, pay-per-click, banners, and unexpected lead sources, like that link John Doe just added to his fan site. And you can likely find a web hosting company that already has Urchin plus the campaign module, and save yourself some money.

I love Urchin. I swear by it far more often than I swear at it, which is a rave review, believe me. Urchin does not pay me any money, give me a commission, send me chocolate, or do anything else to sway my opinion. They probably don't even know I exist, except for that little line item in their books each time my firm buys a license of their software. But in nine years I've not seen better value for traffic and campaign measurement.

Morgan's Bikes: Tracking Conversions, Road Special–style

Morgan knows her dealer-marketing efforts are doing pretty well. But her consumer marketing has a flat tire (sorry, couldn't resist). So she runs a few low-cost pay-per-click ads on Google, persuades her web host to buy Urchin, and starts tracking performance.

She tracks how many consumers complete the Contact Me about the Road Special form on her site, and how many complete the Find a Dealer Near Me form, too. Every time a consumer completes one of those forms, it'll count as a conversion. After one month, her stats reports show her the following for AdWords:

TERMS	CLICKS	CONVERSIONS	COST PER CLICK	TOTAL COST	COST PER LEAD
Road Special	10	5	$0.05	$0.50	$0.10
custom road bikes	200	8	$0.80	$160	$20

Whoa. Those "custom road bikes" leads are costing her a fortune. She only sold three Road Specials last month. But she still doesn't know whether those customers came from either of these PPC ads. And while $20 per lead is pretty steep, she makes about $2,000 per bike. It's probably worth continuing that campaign.

Morgan decides to keep the campaign going, but reduces her AdWords bid for "custom road bikes" to $0.30. That reduces the clicks by a third, but cuts her cost by over 50 percent. That's good.

By keeping track of cost per conversion, Morgan can control her marketing costs, and funnel resources (money) to what appears to be working. She can make sure that these conversations are worth having.

Another Step: Business Intelligence

The final step in observing is to gather business intelligence you can act on. That's a fancy way of saying, "Learn things you didn't know before."

Here's an example: With a little extra programming, Morgan's web guru can add a log of user information — zip code, state, and city — each time a user searches for a dealer. Then she can use that information to guide her marketing in specific parts of the country. Say she discovers that Princeton, N.J., is a hotbed of Road Special interest. She can advertise in the local paper, or even fly there for a special presentation to bike clubs.

There are many opportunities to capture this kind of information on your site:

- **Any geographic search tool**: See the example above.
- **A site search tool**: Log which terms folks search for most often, to determine whether you need to add or reorganize your content.
- **Your shopping cart**: Watch for "bailout," where users place items in their carts but then don't purchase them.
- **E-mail-this-page tools**: If your site has a "Send this page to a friend" tool, measure which pages get forwarded most often. This is a good indicator of interest.
- **E-mail campaigns**: Measure response to different newsletters and messages. Did you get more of or less of a response than expected? Maybe that's telling you something....

Be creative. Web sites, and internet marketing campaigns in general, are an invaluable source of intelligence that most folks ignore.

In any conversation, the more you can observe about your audience's responses, the better you can refine your message (and know whether the conversation's even worth having). In Conversation Marketing, watching those who come to your site, what they look at, and whether they take a desired action lets you do the same. As I said before, the internet offers a unique opportunity to make this kind of observation. Make the most of it.

How to Use Analytics: That Adjusting Thing

So far, I've talked a lot about observing, and not very much about adjusting. Once you start collecting statistics, you have to do a little analysis. Some adjustments are obvious.

- You notice that the most popular page on your site is the page for the Super Widget, so you put information about the Super Widget on your home page.
- Most folks coming to your site come from search engines, so you reduce the money you spend on banner ads.
- Purchases on your site go up 200 percent when your company is mentioned in the news, so you step up PR efforts.

Some are subtler.

- Conversions drop steeply on weekends, but clickthru from pay-per-click ads doesn't, so you "pause" your ad campaigns on Saturday and Sunday to reduce your cost per conversion.
- Visitors keep asking you about selling parts for your product, instead of the whole package, so you begin offering parts on your site.

The possibilities are endless. There are three basic rules, though, that you can apply no matter how simple or sophisticated your web analytics efforts may be:

- **LET IT RIDE.** Don't base adjustment decisions on a single day's data, even if you get 30,000 visitors per day. This is a mistake. Anything — world events, a football game, the World Series, the weather, a new computer virus — can affect traffic patterns locally or worldwide. I generally try to gather at least one week's worth of data before I do anything. And even then I'm careful to look for statistical blips that hurt my ability to see a general trend.
- **PAY ATTENTION.** At the same time, check your stats regularly. Set aside a little time each month (or make sure your internet marketing consultant does) to review how the site's performing and determine whether changes are in order.
- **DEMAND REPORTING.** You probably have a hosting company: they keep your site on a web server, make sure it's running, and give you access so you can make

changes. They should also provide you with web-site traffic statistics, updated daily. There is *no excuse* for not doing so — as I said above, traffic-reporting software is plentiful, and sometimes free. Don't let them tell you that you can't have that data!

Over time, you'll learn the patterns and flow of traffic on your site and be able to recognize when something has a good or bad effect. Then you can adjust accordingly, and keep the conversation going.

Beating the Joneses: How Am I Doing Compared to Everyone Else?

A lot of people want competitive intelligence; they want to see how their site's doing compared to the sites of their competitors.

It is possible to get this kind of information, but you have to take it all with a grain of salt, and sometimes it can cost a pretty penny. I promise not to use any more clichés for at least two paragraphs.

For free, you can use Alexa.com. At the time of this writing, Alexa distributes a tool bar that lets folks do more convenient searching from their desktops. In exchange, Alexa collects data as to which sites those users visit. Alexa then provides that data on its search engine. If you go to Alexa.com and search for a web address, the search results will include a See Traffic Details option. Then you can see the relative traffic rank for that site. By searching on your site and then on your competitors', you can get a very general picture of how you're doing. I say "very general" because Alexa *only* collects data from their toolbar users and users of their search engines. So this isn't a global picture. But it's a good start.

If you have some spare change, consider Hitwise.com and comScore.com. Both use broader measurement techniques to get you a more comprehensive measurement. Each company has something to recommend them, and I'll leave it to their salespeople to convince you. The minimum you'll pay, though, is around $750 for a three-month report.

Conversation Marketing 9

We've come back around now. In this book you've moved from the old, accumulation-based marketing style to the leaner, more efficient selection-based marketing method: Conversation Marketing.

So you're done now, right?

Sorry, no.

Conversation Marketing is a cycle, not a straight line. You have to move through the steps:

- Know the Room
- Dress Appropriately
- Sound Smart
- Make a Connection
- Brag Modestly
- Observe and Adjust

Use what you learned to refine your picture of the room, then start all over again. It's a conversation, remember? It never stops. It pauses now and again, but if you make a connection, and if what you have to say is of value, then there will always be new participants.

Conversation Marketing works. I've used a hypothetical company through this book. But here's a dose of reality.

Real Life

One of my clients (product and names changed to protect the innocent) sells a household product online. The first time he met with me, he told me he was very unhappy with internet marketing and thought he might just give it up. When I asked why, he told me he was paying $15,000 per month in pay-per-click charges. Wow, I said, that's a lot. Are you selling enough to justify that? Yes, he replied, but I don't know if my pay-per-click investment is helping, or if I'm just flushing money down the toilet.

Simple enough. We used conversion-tracking software provided by Yahoo Search Marketing and Google and spent a week watching which terms generated sales, and which ones didn't. At the same time, we surveyed the client's audience, asking potential customers what they looked for in an online resource. The results showed us that most of the terms our client was using were far too broad — imagine someone advertising under the word "snow" when they make skis, and you'll understand what I mean. He was accumulating traffic, not selecting it.

We reduced the scope of his campaigns by removing terms that were neither audience-relevant nor productive. We kept some phrases and terms that were not generating sales, though, if our audience research showed those terms were promising for return customers.

His monthly pay-per-click costs decreased to $6,000, saving him $9,000 per month. Sales went up. When we first proposed our plan to him, he was concerned that reducing the volume of traffic to his site would hurt sales. But by researching his audience and switching to a campaign based on selection, rather than accumulation, we got the best of both worlds.

Another client in a services-based business received plenty of traffic on their site from word of mouth and free search results. They weren't worried about return on investment. But they felt their site wasn't generating any real business. After a little research, we discovered that most folks were going to the site for the wrong reason — to look at pretty photographs and a particular scrolling news ticker that their previous developer had installed on their site.

This was a perfect example of ego-driven design — the designer and client worked together to build something they liked, and got a lot of notoriety for it, but they didn't generate any real business.

We restructured their site around their intellectual assets, and placed on the home page an offer to download a free white paper from the site — after registration. Traffic fell steeply, but they began getting a steady stream of qualified leads to their site. With a measurable conversion goal — the white paper download — in place, we were able to track how efficiently we were selecting traffic. Over time we expanded their online marketing efforts to newsletter sponsorships and other advertising venues — for each campaign, we could measure the results and narrow or refocus our efforts as the data indicated.

Conclusion

Morgan's Bikes: Story Conclusion

There is no conclusion, of course. Morgan is not *done* with internet marketing. But she's now gone through the first cycle. By following the basic rubric of Conversation Marketing, she's built a campaign that includes:

- A web site that caters to her audience in terms of usability, aesthetics, and calls to action, that makes her sound smart.
- An opportunity for her audience to keep in touch.
- Smart online marketing.
- The ability to see every day whether online marketing is working or not.

She knows she's not done, but she's off to a good start.

Select, Converse, Don't Accumulate

If most internet marketers have it all wrong, a few get it right. The success stories — Amazon.com, Google, and Flickr, to name a few — all have one thing in common. They understand their audience, market effectively, and deliver with sensible, functional design. Then they listen to their customers and continuously improve their sites and marketing campaigns.

They make it work by understanding the internet's unique position in the media world as a two-way, mass-communications environment. They learn their audience, design a site that looks just as it should (no one would call Google "pretty"), fill it with great content, and then observe how people respond. Then they fine tune and adapt accordingly.

Having read this book, you may or may not be ready for a career as an internet marketer, but you're definitely ready to talk to one.

Internet marketing can be smarmy, dizzying, confusing, and sometimes downright frustrating. But it can also work brilliantly. I hope this book has moved you a few steps toward the brilliance, and helped you cut through the confusion.

Questions? Rants? Feel as if this was four hours of your life you'll never get back? E-mail me at ian@portentinteractive.com. If your comments are really pithy, I'll even post them to my blog, www.conversationmarketing.com.

Acknowledgments
Where It Comes From

Conversation Marketing grew out of the first six or seven years running my firm, Portent Interactive. It's not easy to tie all of the different facets of a successful internet marketing campaign into a neat, easy-to-explain package — Conversation Marketing tries to do that without oversimplifying or missing the important stuff.

It came from a lot of discussions, internal and with others. If I were forced to name names, I'd say that John Cass (pr.typepad.com) was most instrumental in helping me pull all of this together. His views on PR, marketing, sales, and how they all fit together in an internet-empowered world really guided the process.

It also came from endless guinea-pig sessions with friends and family where I hovered behind them as they browsed the web and fired off questions like, "Why did you click this link and not that one?" Aside from a few disgusted sighs, everyone was a real trooper.

Morgan's Bikes is not, as far as I know, a real company. Morgan is my daughter's name. If there is a real Morgan's Bikes out there, my apologies. And Harrison, don't worry, next time you'll be the star....

ISBN 1412092248

9 781412 092241